Vector

Which Way Does One Turn in a World Going the Wrong Way?

W. D. NICHOLAS

I0453433

Vector

Vector

Which Way Does One Turn in a
World Going the Wrong Way?

WILLIAM NICHOLAS

ARPress
ILLUMINATING IDEAS.
EMPOWERING VOICES

Copyright © 2021 by William Nicholas.

All rights reserved. No part of this publication may be reproduced, distributed, or transmitted in any form or by any means, including photocopying, recording, or other electronic or mechanical methods, without prior written permission of the publisher, except in the case of brief quotations embodied in critical reviews and certain other noncommercial uses permitted by copyright law. For permission requests, write to the publisher, addressed "Attention: Permissions Coordinator," at the address below.

ARPress
45 Dan Road Suite 36
Canton MA 02021

Hotline: 1(888) 821-0229
Fax: 1(508) 545-7580

Ordering Information:
Quantity Sales. Special discounts are available on quantity purchases by corporations, associations, and others. For details, contact the publisher at the address above.

Printed in the United States of America.

ISBN-13   Softcover   979-8-89356-275-0
                      eBook   979-8-89356-274-3

Library of Congress Control Number: 2024903454

In loving memory of
Lisa February 10, 1991- September 25, 2011.

The Fear of the Lord is the beginning of wisdom;
all who follow his precepts have good understanding.
To him belongs eternal praise.
Psalm 111:10

CONTENTS

INTRODUCTION

....

Does it really matter what you believe? Is there more than one way to get to Heaven, or are those crazy Christians, right? Don't all religions lead to God? Is there really such a place as hell?

These and many other questions must be answered. You can be wrong about a lot of things with little or no consequences. But if you are wrong about your "ticket to Heaven," there is no second chance to get it right. Dear friend, whether or not we have ever met, I do care about you, especially about your understanding of things that pertain to your eternal destiny.

As I write there will be certain people in my thoughts, people whom I know to have erroneous ideas about God, or Heaven, or what is required for entry into that realm.

"VECTOR" is defined as a line representing both direction and the magnitude of some force. My first encounter with that word was as an engineer on a 115-foot-long landing craft. This was a part of an exercise that was conducted by our U. S. Navy amphibious fleet.

Our orders were to secure the brass dust cover over the magnetic compass and to turn off the power to the gyrocompass. In effect we were "sailing blind." It was full speed ahead, out to sea. Both the land and the fleet that we were a part of faded into the distance. One could look to the horizon in any direction and see only sky above and water below. Yet we traveled on. It would be futile to turn back without a compass because we could not know where we were headed.

Then the appointed hour came. The chief called the pilot house with the command, "Slow to idle." I repeated that order as I pulled the three throttle levers into the idle position. Shortly a second command was given.

"All stop, send the message." I pulled the throttles into the neutral detent. The radioman, who was at the helm, keyed the radio. Calling the flagship, he identified our vessel and gave the two-word request, "VECTOR ME."

The flagship as well as the other ships of our fleet had known where we were all along. They were equipped to see beyond the horizon. Now we took directions from an unseen guide. A voice from the radio gave us our "vector." We followed the directions of someone that we couldn't see until the other ships were in view.

This book is about finding direction from an unseen Source, a vector that can be trusted. It is about learning to trust that source of guidance. Indeed, it is about building an intimate relationship with that unseen guide.

If there truly is a loving God, who knows everything, and is all powerful, surely, He would be able to show us what He expects of us. If He is not willing to show us what He expects of us, He is not a loving God. If He is not able to tell us, He is nether all- knowing nor all-powerful. But God has made the effort to let us know what He wants from us, and what He wants to do for us. His written "vector" for our lives is so clear and readily available that to fail to find His instructions leaves us "without excuse" (His words, not mine).

The "vector" of which I speak is the Holy Bible. I'm sure that you've heard that science has proved the Bible wrong. The fact is that the Bible is totally reliable. It is the science books which must continually be rewritten due to new findings which render them outdated. The all-knowing God dictated the books of the Bible, so it is always correct and relevant.

There are no scientific errors in the Bible. Although the Bible is not a textbook of science, it makes scientific statements which could not have been known by man at the time it was written because the necessary technology did not exist. Therefore, its author had to possess superior intelligence.

Has it ever occurred to you that the idea that there are many ways to God is irrational? It's not like buying an insurance policy where you select the one that suits your needs. There is only one God, one Heaven, and one set of rules to be observed. Those who don't want to obey God's rules attempt to discredit God's Word, yet they will be judged by the very Word that they deny.

I will begin by showing how we can know beyond a reasonable doubt that the Bible was authored by one with superior intelligence. More than that, one who knew the future, at times hundreds of years in advance of the events foretold. In fact, there are predictions that have not as yet come to pass. But the all-knowing God knew what will happen in the not-so distant future.

There was a man, a very well-known and influential man. His early life was not at all remarkable, yet he applied himself to his work and became rich and famous. He accumulated great wealth and owned lavish homes on both east and west coasts. There were also other homes in locations where he liked to vacation. "He had it all."

Like everyone else will, he died. In an instant, everything that he had accumulated was gone. Everything was left to others who had not worked for this fortune. But worse than that, he went to a place of torment, a place far from the Creator God who loved him and wanted to have a personal relationship with him. Unfortunately, this was his choice. This man had never taken the time to investigate the things that he had heard about his Creator God.

Dear friend, I pray that this will not be your fate. We will test the reliability of the holy Bible by scientific means. Let's get started on our quest to find the true "vector," one who can always be trusted.

A change of plans:

On September 25, 2011, a major tragedy struck our family. Weeks later when I returned to writing I felt it best to rewrite chapter six and rename it chapter one. You will understand why when you turn to the first chapter.

CHAPTER 1

....

Our Little Girl

I
t was just past 8:00 P.M. that late September, Sunday night. Four men came to our door came to our door, two of whom I recognized. They were members of our church, as well as the police department. They wanted to speak with my wife and me alone. We had the kids stay inside while we talked. They asked but a few questions before they broke that awful news: our twenty-year-old daughter had been found dead. She had been murdered.

After a few more questions it was decided that her brother may have some answers that we could not provide. We didn't tell him that Lisa was dead. He was asked if he knew where Lisa's ex- boyfriend lived. He said that he could point out the house but didn't know the address. One of the officers that we knew asked David to go for a ride with him and show him what house that man lived in. That man turned out to be one of the two men who were involved in Lisa's death.

The Miamisburg police worked around the clock to gather evidence and make arrests. They quickly had confessions from both of the suspects. There will be at least two trials and perhaps appeals. The deep wound to our souls will be reopened again and again. We must cling to the assurance that Lisa was an immersed believer. We know that her eternal destiny is in heaven.

Senseless acts of violence such as this are happening all too often. Why has our society become so uncivilized? I believe that it is an unintended consequence of liberalism. Decades ago, our educational system was taken over by those who didn't want to believe in a Creator. If God created us, He owns us, and we need to live by His rules. So, they began to teach that we evolved from lower animals. The idea of evolution has been around for several millennia, but certain people revived and embellished the idea. In truth, evolution is a theory that the facts have failed.

I had not planned to be political, but there are some issues that I find cannot be escaped. First of all, BOTH political parties have some serious flaws. Our problems are much more than political, they are spiritual. Our leadership has removed God from public view and has overruled the very Creator of the universe.

I know that some of the friends that I truly care about are liberals. I don't mean to offend, but certain truths must be stated. YES! There will be democrats in Heaven, but not liberals. How can I say such a thing? Just look at what liberals demand.

Abortion is their "litmus test" for any candidate. Do you really think that abortion is okay with God? According to Scripture God has a purpose for every life, planned or not. In the Old Testament if someone accidentally caused a woman to lose her baby, that person was to be held responsible for that loss, (see Exodus 21:22-25).

We've all heard the battle cry of those who promote abortion: "Keep abortion safe and legal." Fact: before abortion was legalized in1972 the Centers for Disease Control had reported 39 cases of death due to abortions. Two years later there were over 200 deaths due to "safe" abortions. That is greater than a 500% increase. For each death there are many more who are seriously injured.

Homosexual marriage: God made Adam and Eve, NOT Adam and Steve. I'm not saying that it's okay to mistreat those who are homosexual, but they should not get special privileges either. God calls anything from stealing a pack of gum to murder, SIN. But God calls homosexuality, an "abomination." In 1st Corinthians 6:9 there is a list of those who will not go to Heaven. Homosexuals are on that list.

Separation of church and state, Have you ever seen the constitution? That phrase IS NOT THERE! What IS in the constitution, actually the first amendment, is the statement that "congress shall make no law respecting an establishment of religion or prohibiting the free exercise thereof; or abridging the freedom of speech, or of the press; or the right of the people peaceably to assemble, and to petition the Government for a redress of grievances." But liberals do their best to muzzle Judeo-Christian speech while encouraging other religious speech and practice.

Sex outside of marriage is encouraged by liberals. Under God's law, sex is for married couples. You'll read more about the importance of this law in chapter seven. For now, I'll just point out that liberals want to believe that people can't abstain from sex, and we shouldn't expect them to try.

I'm not letting the Republicans off the hook, especially the R.I.N.O.s.

They do their part to spend money that we, as a nation, can't afford. The current administration has spent more than all previous administrations from George Washington to George W. Bush combined and wants to spend even more. (I guess it is fun to spend other people's money). The money that is being spent now is that which will be confiscated from our grandchildren.

No matter if conservative or liberal, it's still human government and, therefore, flawed. Man, from the very beginning has made bad decisions while having good intentions. Eve believed that there was something to be gained by eating the forbidden fruit. We are all paying for that mistake.

So, what does all this have to do with "our little girl"? Everything! When I first begin to write this book, Lisa was a living, breathing, happy young lady with her whole life ahead of her. Her tragic demise is very much linked to the moral decline in our society. The value of human life has been diminished to that of just another animal, or even less. Society protects many animals for various reasons all the while aborting human life as a matter of convenience. Make no mistake about this fact. This nation was founded as a Christian nation. Read the works of the founding fathers. Read what has been chiseled in stone all around the nation's capital. These United States were "a nation under God." History shows that we were blessed by God from the very beginning and continued to be until the people and our government turned away from His Devine leadership.

As I write, this country is in the most serious economic trouble that it has ever seen. I believe that God has removed His blessing from us because of our moral depravity. Psalm 33:12 says, "Blessed is the nation whose God is the Lord, the people he chose for his inheritance." Conversely, Galatians

6:7 says, "Do not be deceived; God cannot be mocked. A man reaps what he sows" That also goes for nations. If you doubt that, just read the history of Israel in the Old Testament. Time after time the nation of Israel would forget all that God had done for them. They would turn away from our God only to get into serious trouble. Only when things got really bad would they repent and turn back to God for help.

Most egregious of all is the secular educational system. Don't get me wrong. I like teachers. I married one. My sister is a teacher, as are many other friends and relatives. The problem is with the system which is controlled by liberal secular humanists. The term "secular humanist" is just a polite way of saying "atheist." But more than just being without God themselves, they want everyone to be like them. They especially don't want the name of Jesus mentioned because someone may be offended by it. Friend, people will be much worse than offended if when they meet Him face to face, they have not accepted Him as their Lord!

Perhaps I am getting ahead of myself. I haven't yet shown you that this Bible that I have been referring to is totally reliable. Most of you have been told that the Bible is full of contradictions, errors, myths and fables. Helping you find the truth, a truth that I searched for, for many years, is the purpose of this book.

As the grandson of an Evangelical United Brethren minister, I knew all the Bible stories. I knew a lot about God, but I didn't really know God. There was a time when I thought that it didn't matter what you believed as long as you did have a belief system. Still, if there was only one God, how could there be more than one why to heaven? I knew that if I studied through a Bible college, I would just get their denominational view of doctrine. I wanted to know what God intended for us to know. Do I know it all now? Far from it. But I do know where and how to find the answers. One could never know all there is to know even if he studied God's Word for a lifetime. I want to help you discover how to find the answers as well.

Before I can help you learn to find these answers, I must first show you that you can trust the source of this information. The Bible claims to be "God breathed." That is, the human writers were told, or, perhaps more accurately, lead to write the things that God wanted to tell you, me, anyone who wanted to understand God's will. The things we need to know to live a life pleasing to our Creator. We can actually get a glimpse of the personality of some of these writers as we read the words they have written. Yet even so, there are no contradictions and no errors in any of its sixty-six books. Ultimately, the author of the Bible was the Creator God Himself.

Admittedly this first chapter will seem a bit disjointed. My task is to try to weave several general truths into an overall paradigm. So, what factors have we put on the table so far? First of all, there is our little girl who was savagely killed. Secondly there are the unintended consequences of liberalism. One must understand that what is an unintended consequence of liberalism is the breakdown of our society. Thirdly, the removal of God from public view is required for liberalism to succeed. As you will come to see throughout the remainder of this book, The Bible is the "owner's manual" for the human race. This will be point number four if you are counting. Contrary to popular belief, the Bible is not out of date, it doesn't need to change because God got it right on the first draft. It is God's guidebook to you, and anyone who wants to understand Him.

The main thrust of this chapter has to do with the moral depravity of our society. If you watch any news program or read a newspaper you know full well that crimes of every type are rampant. There are wars going on all around this world. I must reiterate what has been said for many years. "If God doesn't bring judgment on these United States, He owes Sodom and Gomorrah an apology."

When I mention Sodom and Gomorrah, I am not limiting my thinking only of homosexuality. I include abortion, pornography, adultery, theft, not only by common people but also by our political leaders, perhaps especially by our political leaders. When a certain president was caught doing sexual acts with an intern in the oval office, the media tried to say that that wasn't sex. Excuse me! Unless one is a doctor performing an examination, when one person is touching the genitals of another, that is sex. The result of this redefining of terms has encouraged many teens to indulge in oral sex in the belief that it really isn't sex. However, you want to define it, it still allows the transfer of sexually transmitted diseases.

When the current administration was appointing cabinet officials there were many who had hundreds of thousands of dollars in tax problems. The media called it "an oversight." Had you or I been found with even a small amount of undeclared income, it would be called "tax evasion," and we would face time in prison for that.

We common folk likely can't get inside information on the stock market, but if we could, it would be illegal to use such information. Our government leaders can and do get and use such information and enrich themselves greatly.

Are you beginning to get the message that all is not well in these United States? There is a whole lot more that could be said about the moral condition of this country. Liberalism is all about defining deviancy down. Changing words and phrases to hide the true meanings, making them seem less objectionable. God must be redefined as being a myth which is believed only by the unenlightened. It's okay to believe in a little "g" god as long as it doesn't interfere with your allegiance to government. To a liberal or an R.I.N.O., government IS god. If you have any need at all you are to look to the government to fulfill your needs.

In order for the government to give to one person, it then must first take away from someone else. They don't have a dime unless they take it away from people who have earned it. So why can't they take it from the rich people? According to those who have done the math if you took every dollar over $200,000.00 from all those rich people it would only fund the government for a few months. At that point we would be up the proverbial creek without a paddle. You could only confiscate those funds once, then there would be no rich people from which to get those funds again. Worse than that, there would be no rich who would be able to hire new workers.

Has anyone ever tried this liberal approach to funding and spending before? Yes, the Soviet Union, Great Brittan, France, Grease just to name a few. You are aware of what has happened in those countries aren't you? "But those are socialist countries," you say. Right! Let me set you straight on the "isms." Liberalism is a kind word for socialism. Socialism is a springboard to Communism. I know, that's an over simplification. When you get right down to the real difference between the "isms," A Communist will defend his boarders and support his military. You are not likely to find a liberal doing those things.

The common thread among the isms is that they seek to control the general population. This can only be done by making the people dependent on the government for their survival. How do you make them dependent? Take away their jobs. Just look around, many of the new jobs are government jobs. Those jobs depend on the government, too. Some of these new government jobs were created to police the regulations which limit the ability of private business to operate, expand, or hire. There will be 16.000 agents to enforce Obamacare.

Let's not forget "Fast and Furious." I don't mean the movie, but the attempt of our administration to kill the second amendment. The plan was to let drug dealers get their hands on guns at American dealers, then, when the guns were caught in criminal hands the case could be used to abolish the second amendment. Fortunately, their plan failed, but in the process, a few hundred lives were taken with those guns. This is how liberals work. It is all a power struggle, and they know that they must disarm the American public before they can reach their goal. That's the way it's been in every country which has gone socialist. It's all about power, and only the "chosen few" who are in the top levels of government will be rich.

Update: The liberal lapdog news media has tried to say that Fast and Furious began in the Bush administration. Not so. Between 2005 and 2007 there was a mission called "Wide Receiver." This operation consisted of 400 assault weapons which had tracking devices and with the full knowledge and cooperation of the Mexican government. The operation was ended because the criminals had discovered the tracking devises and removed them.

Fast and Furious began in 2009 with 2000 assault weapons without tracking devises and without the knowledge of the Mexican government. It was expected that there would be casualties, over 200 Mexicans and at least one American Boarder Guard were killed with those weapons. This was intended by our liberal (whatever it takes to ban guns) government.

Socialism has failed everywhere it's been tried. Still, those who have been indoctrinated in leftist philosophy think that they can make socialism work. Is Marx the kind of man you really want to follow as a role model? Marx lived his socialist philosophy to the extent that four of his seven children, (eight if you count his illegitimate child), died due to the poverty that they had to endure. One of Marx's friends described his filthy home as "a pigsty." Karl Marx was too lazy to get off of his (idealism) and go to work and feed his family.

Why do I spend so much ink on the isms when I started the chapter telling about our little girl? That, dear friend, is because the isms are at the very heart of the cause of her death. The isms breed the mindset of those who could take the life of another person without provocation. The isms remove the barrier to killing one who is no threat to you. How do they open such doors? Hang on. That will all be coming together in due course.

As previously stated, liberalism has taken over the educational system. This is always at the heart of socialist governments. Indoctrinate the young in the liberal ideology, the younger the better. (Why do you think they have pre-school)? Do not allow the mention of a big "G" God. The only higher power that kids should believe in is, (guess who) the government. Have you noticed that non-government schools such as private or Christian schools always produce higher achieving students? Even so, the government, in its infinite wisdom doesn't like any competition. Not even if they do get better results. The government doesn't want smarter students; they are not as easy to control. Furthermore, those schools don't have union teachers who pay dues that can be used to fund liberal campaigns.

Power and control are the name of the game. The power to tax is the power to control. I am not advocating any kind of rebellion. I look to a higher power, the Creator God. I know that He is ultimately in control, and He may well be ready to let this nation go down the tubes. Hey, we've turned our backs on Him. Why would God want to help us out of this mess? A few decades ago, we were Israel's sword. The present administration is willing to throw Israel under the bus.

Know this, God will bless those who bless Israel, and He will curse those who curse Israel. Let's not ever forget, Jesus is a Jew.

Alright already. What's so bad about the schools-other than the fact that they are graduating students who can't read above a 5th grade level, and who can't make change or speak proper English? Let's start, the censorship of the thanksgiving story for one thing. There is rewriting of the discovery of North America, and the founding of our country for another. Above all let's not forget the revising of history so that children don't know that this country was founded as a Christian nation. No, we were not to have an official religion, but the principles were based on those found in the Bible.

Why have the politicians pushed God out of the way? Power and control, of course. Rights come from God, a fact which is acknowledged in the wording of our constitution. But if you will think about it, the current administration doesn't care much about the constitution. It is not the point of this book to carry on at length about this administration; others have been doing that in volumes. I will instead continue on the education system as that leads directly to the cause of our moral decline.

The liberal agenda requires that God goes away. Although God isn't going anywhere, when kids are indoctrinated with a godless view of life and pseudo-science, they are on their way down the slippery slope. Soon they will question any belief in God which they may have had. Should these young ones go on to college some godless professor will make it his duty to see that they are atheists before they graduate. Fact: 80 % of Christian students who attend college will leave their faith. The problem is not with the Christian faith but with the false teaching to which they are subjected in college.

What is true, what is false, what is science, what is pseudo- science? These issues will be covered at length throughout the remainder of this book. For now, we need to finish weaving these items together.

The young and impressionable must be caused to question anything they may have been told about God. Teach them that we are the result of a cosmic accident. Teach them that we are only highly evolved animals. Well, isn't that what you were taught? Personally, I was never gullible enough to buy that evolution stuff. I grew up on a farm and I knew where animals came from. When I was told that the giraffe was a horse-like animal which got caught in a long dry spell and his neck got longer so he could eat tree leaves, I knew better. I could see that this was not a reasonable explanation.

Even while in junior high I could see major flaws with the whole evolutionary story. While some of the answers were obvious to me, there were other issues which I was unable to reconcile. It was years later that I discovered a source of scientific information which not only answered my questions but fit beautifully with the Scripture.

The story goes something like this; "Nothing exploded and from that explosion came everything." Wow, what great logic! Then all of those gases cooled and condensed to form stars. Never mind that there is no law of science that would allow that to happen. When it comes to evolution, the students are to check their minds at the door. Don't ever question anything; just accept it as it is told to you.

In our public schools evolution is taught as fact. No other view may be mentioned (brainwashing). The student is to accept that we have evolved from some lower form of life and that we are just an accident of time and chance. We are taught that life is a matter of "survival of the fittest." We don't need a God to explain how we got here; therefore, there are no rules. Without God looking over our shoulder we are free to do whatever seems good to us. The problem with that thinking comes when someone else wants what you have, and they have the ability to take that thing away from you. Without God there is no basis for morality. The only law is survival of the fittest.

In case you didn't notice, all of the factors that I was weaving together are now complete. The Creator God has been kicked out of all public places. We enjoy a new kind of freedom, the freedom to do as we please until we don't, please someone who has the ability to stop us. In a Godless society there is no moral ground for laws or punishment. Without a God, abortion is just a choice. Now that killing babies is legal, (no, I don't mean a fetus), there are some who want to end the lives of the old and infirm.

The whole idea of abortion has cheapened human life to the point that for some, the thought of killing another person is no big deal. Some will even kill just to see what it feels like; they place no value on life. They believe that we are just animals, and they act like animals. One of the killers at Columbine High School wore a shirt which said, "Survival of the Fittest."

I hold to God's view of human life. Our little girl, Lisa's death was far more significant than our personal loss. Every person has significance in God's eyes. God has created every one of us for a special purpose. Psalm 139:13-14 reads: "For you created my inmost being; you knit me together in my mother's womb. I praise you because I am fearfully and wonderfully made; your works are wonderful, I know that full well."

Every human soul that has ever walked this earth was created to serve a special purpose for the Creator God. No one has the right to cut a life short. Okay, someone who opposes capital punishment just read that and said "see, we can't execute people." Wrong! God also provided for that in Genesis 9:6, as well as other places. "Whoever sheds the blood of man, by man shall his blood be shed; for in the image of God has God made man." Just as is true with many other laws, capital punishment is authorized in God's Word.

The county prosecutor has made Lisa's death a capital case. According to the laws of the state of Ohio the death penalty is appropriate. It is also appropriate according to the Word of God. Personally, I must trust that God will see that justice is done. I must leave the matter in His capable hands. "Vengeance is mine says the Lord."

Of all the things that a parent may think of that could happen to one of their children, murder is not on the list. The things that we try to guard against are scraped knees, bloody noses and broken bones. We may be concerned about auto accidents, especially when they get that all-liberating driver's license. Whatever concerns we have for our children, we never think of one of them being murdered. Why doesn't it cross our minds? We hear of another shooting or a stabbing on every newscast. But that is always someone else, in another town; it's not the sort of thing that happens to us.

Friend, we live in a fallen world. Modern society is a Godless society. So long as our educational system keeps turning out students who believe that they are just animals, we can expect more of the same. So, what sort of advice would I give you? Keep on reading; you need to know the truth about who we are, why we are here and what we are supposed to be doing while we are here. You need to know what the best proof is that the Bible is reliable. And you need to know that the troubles that we are now facing were predicted long ago in the Bible.

I sincerely pray that you will never have to go through what we are now experiencing. For our family this is only the beginning. But we have our faith to hold on to. We trust God to help us through whatever is yet to come. I wonder if the families of the killers know God. It must be a terrible thing to have a child on trial for murder. I cannot help but feel compassion for those families.

At this point I'm sure that readers who don't have "faith" are thinking "How can you have faith in a God who would allow your child to be killed?" Faith is a living, growing thing. It always starts out as something small and fragile, yet it grows as one sees more and more evidence of the loving provision of God. Honestly, I have seen my own faith grow in the weeks since.

It is a part of human nature to question God when trouble comes our way. After due consideration I find that it is the height of arrogance to question the will of the Creator of the universe. Humanly, we have the will and the right to defend our family and friends. As a Navy veteran and one who was trained by the Ohio State Highway Patrol, had I been there when Lisa was attacked the outcome would certainly have been different. But that was not to be, I was not there. But the God who loves her was there and Lisa is with Him now and forever more.

During the first few days after the tragedy, I would hear people say that God will bring something good from this. I knew that they were right, but I didn't have a clue what that could be. First, I saw that the entire community was deeply affected. Total strangers would come to our door to express their feeling or to tell us that they would be praying for us. Some wanted to make donations. Others brought in food. Our church has been absolutely fabulous, caring and supportive.

At times it feels a bit uncomfortable to accept gifts from people that you don't really know. In truth, by graciously accepting their gifts it is helping them to heal as well. These people feel a sense of loss as well. Their neighborhood has been violated; evil has come close, too close to their families.

I recall an evening a few days after the murder when we had a house full of people. I was standing on the front porch when a lady whom I didn't know came up to express her condolences. She told me how she had come to know the Lord and she wanted to leave her phone number and address in case we thought of something she could do to help. Months passed My wife, Linda, sent her a card and a note at Christmas time. The reply was a shocker. During those three months she had been diagnosed with cervical cancer, had surgery and was scheduled for radiation treatments. I immediately put her on my prayer list. Why do I mention her? Three months before, she was praying for us. Now we see the need to be praying for her.

It is God's will that we believers care about one another. We are also to care about non-believers and do what we can to help them come to what I call "the saving knowledge" of Jesus Christ. And so it is that as you read on you will be presented with that knowledge and hopefully you too will begin a relationship with the Creator of the universe, and lover of your soul.

CHAPTER 2

....

Proof From Prophecy

W hat sets the Bible apart from all other (so called) religious books is prophecy. There are many who make predictions about the future. Some are even right as much as 20% of the time. Sometimes one has to stretch the facts a bit to say that these predictions are right. I can show you hundreds of prophecies that were right to the most intricate detail. These are found in the Holy Bible. It's one thing to make such a statement. Let's take a look at some of these prophecies and see how accurate they are.

There are about 2500 prophecies in the Bible. Of these, some 2000 have been fulfilled exactly as they were predicted. The remaining 500 are for the future. I and many others believe that they are for the near future. The amazing accuracy of the fulfillment of past prophecies makes it clear that we can count on the rest to be 100% accurate, too.

The mighty city of Babylon, nearly 200 miles square, had a double wall 330 feet high and 90 feet thick. Two Bible prophets predicted its doom. Isaiah 13:17-22 and Jeremiah 51:26, 43 said that travelers would avoid its ruins and that the city would never be rebuilt. The stones of the city would not even be moved and used for building material. The prophets were both 100% right. The odds of chance fulfillment equal 1 in 1,000,000,000.

Jeremiah predicted, (Jeremiah 49:15-20), that Edom, (a part of Jordan), would become a barren and uninhabited wasteland. At that time, it was a fertile land and had much water. Today it is as Jeremiah predicted. The odds of chance fulfillment equal 1 in 100,000.

Of special interest are the Messianic prophecies. That term refers to well over one hundred predictions found in the Old Testament. Some of these prophecies date back over 1,000 years before Christ and are found in the Dead Sea scrolls and the Septuagint. The Jews had been watching for their Messiah for centuries, yet when He arrived, most of them missed Him. Although there were over a hundred prophecies to guide them in their search, they still missed the most important event of their times.

Did God need to go to "plan B"? Of course not, He is outside of time and able to foresee what His people would do when their Messiah came. This, of course is why the Bible prophecies are always totally right. God knows the future and told His prophets what to write. Today we can use fulfilled prophecy as evidence for the reliability of the Bible. Therefore, the things prophesied to happen in the future are sure to come to pass as well.

Around 700 B.C. the prophet Micah predicted that the tiny village of Bethlehem would be the birthplace of Christ. The odds of chance fulfillment equal 1 in 100,000.

In the fifth century B.C. the prophet Zechariah said that the Messiah would be betrayed for the price of a slave which was 30 pieces of silver. This money would be used to buy the potter's field, a place to bury poor aliens. The odds of chance fulfillment equal 1 in 1,000,000.

Rather than list all of these prophecies, (which would take more pages than I intend to write), let's see what just seven of them would do to the odds of chance fulfillment.

1. Jesus would be a descendant of David.	Odds: 1 in 10,000
2. He would be born in Bethlehem. Odds:	1 in 100,000
3. He would be a miracle worker.	Odds: 1 in 100,000
4. Jesus would present Himself as King while riding a donkey.	Odds: 1 in 1,000,000
5. He would be betrayed by a friend for 30 pieces of silver.	Odds: 1 in 1,000,000
6. Jesus would be crucified. (a means of execution not invented when prophesied.)	Odds: 1 in 1,000,000
7. Date that Christ would first present Himself as King linked to decree by Artaxerxes.	Odds: 1 in 1,000,000

Total probability without God's intervention: 10 to the 38th power which is, 1 in a 100 billion, billion, billion, billion. Remember, this is only seven of more than a hundred prophecies. Talk about a "SURE THING," this is why it is said that prophecy is the "atheists nightmare."

There are those who would say that Jesus just tried to fulfill all of those prophecies himself. Okay, how does one get born in the right town? And how could he arrange to be born of a virgin? As an infant he could not influence the king to try to kill all the boy babies in that region. That's when his parents took him to Egypt for safety, just as prophesied. The list of things that he could not have controlled goes on and on.

Some would like to believe that His body was stolen from the tomb. Those who had Him crucified thought that this could happen, so they had Roman guards posted to prevent that vary possibility. Don't overlook the fact that these guards were seasoned warriors. Furthermore, if they let the one that they were guarding get away, their own lives would likely be taken.

Another inconsistency with the "stolen body theory" is that in that culture, women were, at best, second class citizens. If someone were going to make up a story, they would not make women the first witnesses to an event when women were not even allowed to testify in court.

After His resurrection Jesus was seen by as many as five hundred people at one time. These people were still alive when the record of these events was written, and they would have protested if it were not true. Let's not forget that most of the disciples were executed for their testimony that Jesus was resurrected from the dead. Do you really think that they would go to their own deaths to preserve a lie?

There are also some prophecies that have had recent fulfillment. Isaiah 41: 12-14, (written about 700 B.C.) predicted that Israel would prevail over its enemies. Since 1948 when Israel was re-established as a nation it has been attacked by much larger countries. Each time it has prevailed.

Amos 9:11-13, (written about 750 B.C.) said that "the ruins of Israel would be rebuilt." This has been going on during the past 100 years. Modern farming and irrigation have turned this once barren land into productive farmland. Israel is now a source of food for many countries.

Ezekiel 36:11, (written between 593 and 571 B.C.) prophesied prosperity for modern-day Israel. Over the past century Jews from all around the world have returned to Israel and have been rebuilding the country once again. In 1999 Israel had the highest per capita Gross Domestic Product of any nearby country even though the surrounding countries have many oil resources.

I understand that prophecy is not the favorite subject of most people. I am much more comfortable with scientific evidence myself. So, since I'm a nice guy I'll excuse those readers who would rather not read the following list of prophecies. For those who want to learn more – I will give you an opportunity to do a more in-depth study.

The first Messianic prophecy is found in Genesis 3:15. "And I will put enmity between you and the woman, and between your offspring and hers; he will crush your head, and you will strike his heel."

Say what? Okay, the woman and the snake won't get along. And it will be that way through all generations. "Strike his heel," refers to the crucifixion. "Crush your head" refers to the fact that when Christ returns, He will put an end to Satan's rule and deception. The fulfillment of this prophecy is found in Galatians 4:4-5. "But when the time had fully come, God sent his Son, born of a woman, born under law, to redeem those under the law, that we might receive the full rights of sons."

Admittedly that verse from Genesis was a little difficult to understand. It takes some time and study to begin to learn prophetic language. As I list the following scripture references, I will put the ones which are easy to understand in brackets. I do want you to understand enough of these prophecies to realize that God is the true author of the Bible. At the beginning of each reference will be the prophetic passage followed by the passage telling of the fulfillment.

Genesis 12:3; 18:18; The Messiah will be a descendant of Abraham through whom everyone on earth will be blessed. Acts 3; 25-26.

Genesis 49: 10 The Messiah will be a descendant of Judah.
Matthew 1:2 and Luke 3: 33.
Deuteronomy 18:15-19; The Messiah will be a prophet, like Mosses. Acts 3:22-23.
Psalm 27; The Messiah will be the Son of God. Matthew 3: 17, Mark 1:11 and Luke 3: 22.

[Psalm 16:10-11; The Messiah will be raised from the dead, (resurrected). Matthew 28:5-9; Mark 16:6; Luke 24:4-7; John 20:11-16 [Acts 1:3 & 2:32].

[Psalm 22 contains 11 prophecies – not all listed here]. The Messiah's crucifixion experience, Matthew 27:34-50 and John 19:17-30.

Psalm 22:7; The Messiah will be sneered at and mocked. Luke 23:11, 35-39.

[Psalm 22:16; The Messiah will be pierced through His hands and feet. Luke 23:33 and 24:36-39; [John 19:18 and 20: 19-20, 24-27].

[Psalm 22:17 and 34:20]; The Messiah's bones will not be broken. (a person's legs were usually broken after being crucified to speed up their death). [John 19:31-33, 36].

[Psalm 22:18]; Men will gamble for the Messiah's clothing.
Matthew 27:35, Mark 15:24, Luke 23, 34, [John 19:23-24].
Psalm 35:11; The Messiah will be accused by false witnesses.
Matthew 26:59-60; and Mark 14:56-57.
Psalm 35:19 and 69:4; The Messiah will be hated without a cause.
John 15:23-25.

[Psalm 41:9]; The Messiah will be betrayed by a friend. [John 13:18, 21].

[Psalm 68:18]; The Messiah will ascend to heaven and sit at the right hand of God. [Luke 2451; Acts 1:9] acts 2:33-35; 3:20-21; 5:31-32; 7:55-56; Romans 8:34; Ephesians 1:20-21; Colossians 3:1; Hebrews 1:3; 8:1; 10:12; 12:2; 1Peter 3:22......

Psalm 69:21; The Messiah will be given vinegar and gall to drink. Matthew 27:34; Mark 15:23; John 19:29-30.

Psalm 72:10-11; Great kings will pay homage and tribute to the Messiah. Matthew 2:1-11.

Psalm 118:22-23; and Isaiah 28:16; The Messiah is a "stone the builders rejected" who will become the "head cornerstone." Matthew 21: 42, 43; Acts 4:11; Ephesians 2:20; 1 Peter 2:6-8.

Psalm 132:11 and Jeremiah 23:5-6 and 33; 15-16; The Messiah will be a descendant of king David. Luke 1:32-33.

[Isaiah 7:14]; The Messiah will be born of a virgin. [Matthew 1;18-25; Luke 1:26-335].

Isaiah 9:1-7; The Messiah's first spiritual work will be in Galilee. Matthew 4:12-16.

Isaiah 35:5-6; The Messiah will make the blind see, the deaf hear, etc. Matthew 11:3-6; John 11:47; and many other passages.

[Isaiah 50:6]; The Messiah will be beaten, mocked, and spat upon. [Matthew 26:67 and 27:26-31].

[Isaiah 53:3]; The Messiah will be rejected. [Matthew 27:20-26; Mark 15:8-14; Luke 23:18-23; John 19:14-15].

[Isaiah 53:5-9]; The Messiah will be killed. [Matthew 27: 50, Mark 15: 37-39, Luke 23:18-23, John 19:30].

[Isaiah 53:7]; The Messiah will be silent in front of His accusers. [Matthew 26; 62-63; and 27:12-14].

Isaiah 53:9; The Messiah will be buried with the rich. Matthew 27:59-60; Mark 15:46; Luke 23:52-53; John 19:38-42.

[Isaiah 53:12]; The Messiah will be crucified with criminals. [Matthew 27:38; Mark 15:27; Luke 23:32-33].

Isaiah 55:3-4 and [Jeremiah 31:31-34]; The Messiah is part of the new and everlasting covenant. Matthew 26:28 Mark 14:24; Luke 22:20; [Hebrews 8:6-13].

Isaiah 59:16; The Messiah will be our intercessor. Hebrews 9:15.

Daniel 9:26; The Messiah will come at a specific time. Galatians 4:4; and Ephesians 1:10.

[Micah 5:2]; The Messiah will be born in Bethlehem. [Matthew 2:1 and Luke 2:4-7].

[Zechariah 9:9] ; The Messiah will enter Jerusalem riding a donkey. [Matthew 21:11].

[Zechariah 11:12-13]; The Messiah will be sold for 30 pieces of silver. [Matthew 26:15 with Matthew 27:3-10].

[Zechariah 13:7]; The Messiah will be forsaken by His disciples, [Matthew 26:31, 56].

Malachi 3:1; The Messiah will enter the Temple with authority. Matthew 21:12; and Luke 19:45.

Okay! If you have looked up all of those Scriptures, you deserve a short break. The important thing is that you see that the Bible is totally accurate and can be trusted. I'm sure that you've heard otherwise from some people, but, in truth, the Bible has been proven accurate and trustworthy.

Prophecy, "the atheist's nightmare," has given us reason to be fully confidant in the Bible. Obviously, the reason for its accuracy is because it is "God breathed." That is, God directed those who wrote the various books of the Bible as to what they should write. God, being outside of time and able to see what will happen in the future, was able to tell them exactly what was going to happen in great detail. It was God's intention that prophecy would give His people confidence and help others to see that His Word is reliable.

But, Bill, hasn't science proven the Bible wrong? <u>NO, NOT</u> <u>AT ALL!</u>

In fact, the greatest portion of this book will be dealing with that very subject. We will touch on it in the next chapter, and there is much more to come.

There have always been those who don't want to believe in God. Unfortunately, they are in control of the education system, so they edit what is taught at all levels of learning. In 1925 the A.C.L.U. talked a teacher named John Scopes into allowing him to be tried for teaching evolution in the classroom. At that time there was little known about creationism. The much-publicized event, often called the "Scopes Monkey Trial," was in reality an attempt to get evolution into the school system. Then, they "just wanted to teach it alongside of creation." Today they will not allow creation to be mentioned in public schools. The fact is that if the two viewpoints were compared side by side, evolution would be rejected by most thinking people.

Let me explain why I decided to write this book. It's all because of this Jewish carpenter that I know. You may know Him; His name is Jesus. He is the one who suggested that I write a book. What would I write about? Obviously, it had to be about Biblical Creation; that is what I've been studying for the last forty years. Still, it had to be more than that. I have a large library on the subject, what could I add to what those professionals have written? Then the Jewish Carpenter (Jesus) reminded me that I have also studied a lot of prophecy and that prophecy is God's way of showing us that His Word is true.

Okay! Add that to the call to tell my friends about the "saving knowledge of Christ" and we have a reason to get started. He has made it very clear to me that we are all unique individuals, created to serve Him in some special way. We have different backgrounds, different educational experiences, as well as different work experiences. We are all uniquely created to serve our Creator in a way that He needs. His call depends less on your ability than on your availability. Are you willing to serve Him?

I realize that much of what I am telling you is going to be some pretty heavy stuff. Your relationship with your Creator is serious business. I would like you to know that I like to joke around as much as anyone does. Let's lighten up for a moment while I tell you about an elderly couple, I mean very elderly, who died at nearly the same time. They walked through the streets of heaven hand in hand. The wife said, "Isn't it beautiful here?" Her husband replied, "Yes dear, it certainly is."

"Have you noticed that all the people seem to be very happy?" the wife asked. "Yes dear" the man replied, "they are joyous, and just think, if you hadn't insisted that we eat all that oat bran we could have come here ten years ago."

CHAPTER 3

....

Is It Real, Or Is It Myth?

Allow me if you will, to set the stage in the theater of your mind. Picture a medieval castle set high on a hill. There is a pathway winding its way down the hill and ending on the banks of a placid lake. Along the pathway walks a beautiful princess. As she walks along, she seems to be looking for something, "special."

As she reaches the banks of the lake, she sees a little green frog. She picks him up and looks intently into his eyes. And then, she leans forward, she kisses the frog on his lips! SUDDENLY,,,, in a shower of stars the frog is transformed into a handsome prince!!!!

Now if you believe that a frog can be transformed into a prince in an instant, that's a fairy tale. HOWEVER,,,, if you believe that it takes a few million years, that's evolution!!!!

Yes, dear friend, evolution is more fable than fact, a fairy tale. As some of my colleagues like to say, "Evolution is a faith that the facts have failed." As you will see as we proceed, for every "answer" the evolutionists give, they only raise more questions.

When we look at the evidence based on what one would expect to find as a Biblical Creationist, it all fits very well. It's like seeing the hand of God as He brought everything into existence. So, what do we see when we look at day one of creation as written in God's Word? Genesis 1:1-2 states that "In the beginning God created the heavens and the earth. Now the earth was formless and empty, darkness was over the surface of the deep, and the Spirit of God was hovering over the waters," (New International Version).

There are some who claim that the phrase, "formless and empty" refers to a world that had previously been destroyed and was now to be recreated. Frankly there is little to no evidence, Scriptural or geological, to support this idea. Scripture says that God created, not recreated, the world in six days. Had the earth, "formless and empty," existed before the first day of creation week, that would have added to the length of the week.

What if we accept these first two verses at face value? It would be like a potter who puts a lump of clay on his potter's wheel. It's "without form." It will require the hand of the potter to give it "form" and purpose.

Genesis 1:3; "And God said, 'Let there be light.' and there was light. God saw that the light was good, and he separated the light from the darkness." It doesn't say what the source of that light was. We are never told what it was. The following verses go on to say that God divided the light from the darkness making day and night. But hang on! If there was day and night the earth must have been turning, and the light coming from one point in the heavens.

Genesis 1:5; "God called the light 'Day' and the darkness he called 'night.' And there was evening, and the morning— the first day."

Genesis 1:6-7; "And God said, 'Let there be an expanse between the waters to separate water from water.' So, God made the expanse and separated the waters under the expanse from the waters above it. And it was so."

The "expanse" is called the "firmament" in other translations. It is the atmosphere from which we breathe, and in which birds fly. The waters above the expanse may refer to a water vapor canopy which some believe surrounded the earth before the great flood. While you won't find reference to this vapor canopy in your high school textbook, even some evolutionists believe in this possibility.

When you read the first chapters of the book of Genesis you see long life spans into many hundreds of years. The champion of all was Methuselah, (Genesis 5:27), who lived to be 969 years old. When you read about the life spans of people after the flood you will notice that the life spans begin to drop off abruptly. Why would this be? Because the protective vapor canopy had collapsed as a part of the deluge. Therefore, solar radiation would be much more damaging to the life forms on this earth.

Is this proof of creation? No, not exactly. But when you take your little shovel and start digging you will see that the evidence fits best with what you read in the Bible.

Genesis 1:8; God called the expanse 'sky.' And there was evening, and the morning— the second day."

Genesis 1:9-10; "And God said, 'Let the waters under the sky be gathered together to one place, and let dry ground appear.' And it was so. God called the dry ground 'land,' and the gathered waters he called 'seas.' And God saw that it was good."

Question! If the waters were in one place, being one big ocean, wouldn't the land also have to be in one place? Being one big continent? I'm not the first to ask that question. If you look at a globe you can see that the east coast of the America has a very similar shape to that of Western Europe and Africa. It's like they had just split apart. Geologically the materials are much the same on each side of the Atlantic.

Again, I'm not the first to ask that question. It is quite logical to believe that there was only one continent until the time of the great flood. That view fits very well with the Scripture. It also explains how, when and why that continent was split apart. We'll look into that issue in more detail later.

Genesis 1:11-13; "Then God said, 'Let the land produce vegetation: seed-bearing plants and trees on the land that bear fruit with seed in it, according to their various kinds.' And it was so. The land produced vegetation: plants bearing seed according to their kinds and trees bearing fruit with seed in it according to their kinds. And God saw that it was good. And there was evening, and there was morning— the third day."

In these verses we are introduced to a new phrase, "according to their kind." We'll be seeing that phrase a number of times in this chapter. This is as close as the Bible comes to using the modern term, "DNA." As you will see, DNA is the "blueprint" for "after its kind." You can't build a skyscraper with a blueprint for a ranch style house. The necessary information is simply not there. It's much the same with DNA. If the blueprint contained in a seed is for a type of grass. That is what will come from that seed. You can count on it every time. There are many varieties of grass and if you mix different varieties you can come up with a new one BUT! It will still be grass. We'll discuss this more in chapter 5.

Genesis 1:14-19; "And God said, 'Let there be lights in the expanse of the sky to separate the day from the night and let them serve as signs to mark seasons and days and years and let them be lights in the expanse of the sky to give light on the earth'. And it was so. God made two great lights- the greater light to govern the day and the lesser light to govern the night. He also made the stars. God set them in the expanse of the sky to give light on the earth, to govern the day and the night, and to separate light from the darkness. And God saw that it was good. And there was evening, and there was morning— the fourth day."

There is something called the "day - age" theory. It is a belief that the "DAYS" in Genesis are actually "AGES", long periods of time rather than 24-hour days. If that were true, there is a big problem. How could there be trees, grass and other vegetation for long ages without the sun? Notice also that the bees haven't been created yet. Bees are necessary for fruit trees to bear fruit as well as to pollinate other vegetation.

Genesis 1:20-23; "And God said, 'Let the water teem with living creatures, and let birds fly above the earth across the face of the expanse of the sky.' So, God created the great creatures of the sea and every living and moving thing with which the water teems, according to their kinds, and every winged bird according to its kind. And God saw that it was good. God blessed them and said, 'Be fruitful and increase in number and fill the water in the seas, and let the birds increase on the earth.' And there was evening, and there was morning— the fifth day."

Again, we see the phrase, "according to their kind." Have you noticed, every day is marked by the phrase, "there was evening and morning," and followed by a number? What better way to say that these are 24-hour days?

Genesis 1:24-25; "And God said, 'Let the land produce living creatures according to their kinds: livestock, creatures that move along the ground, and wild animals, each according to its kind.' And it was so. God made the wild animals according to their kinds, the livestock according to their kinds, and all the creatures that move along the ground according to their kinds. And God saw that it was good."

There are those among us who think that God should have quit right there. In their opinion the next creature that God created has been the downfall of all creation. Yet it was God's intention that this creature would be the STEWARD of all creation.

Genesis 1; 26-28; "Then God said, 'Let us make man in our image, in our likeness, and let them rule over the fish of the sea and the birds of the air, over the livestock, over all the earth, and over all the creatures that move along the ground.' So, God created man in His own image, in the image of God he created him; male and female he created them. God blessed them and said to them, 'Be fruitful and increase in number; fill the earth and subdue it. Rule over the fish of the sea and the birds of the air and over every living creature that moves on the ground."

Let's examine this a little at a time. "Let US make man in OUR image." Clearly there is more than one PERSON involved. As we read elsewhere in the Scripture, God is "triune," three individuals who are all equally God. They do take on different roles, Father, Son, and Holy Spirit.

Next, we see that God says, "let them rule over all the fish of the sea, over the birds of the air, and over the cattle, over all the earth..." Don't miss the fact that God gave stewardship of the earth and all that is in it to guess who! MAN! That, of course, means that we have an awesome responsibility to our Creator God. We are charged with the maintenance of our environment. We must keep it as clean as possible. We must not waste the resources that God has given us. At the same time, these resources are here for our use. Let's use them wisely.

Genesis 1:29-31; "Then God said, 'I give you every seed-bearing plant on the face of the whole earth and every tree that has fruit with seed in it. They will be yours for food. And to all the beasts of the earth all the birds of the air and all the creatures that move on the ground—everything that has the breath of life in it—I give every green plant for food.' And it was so. God saw all that He had made, and it was very good. And there was evening, and there was morning— the sixth day."

Did you catch that? God gave us fruit and veggies to eat. No burgers, no steaks, no fish, no chicken, not even an opossum. Are we required to be vegetarians? NO! That was before the flood. Later in Genesis 9:3-4 God told Noah that, "Everything that lives and moves will be food for you. Just as I gave you the green plants, I now give you everything. But you must not eat meat that has its lifeblood still in it." Why the change? Obviously there had been a major change in the environment, atmosphere, and dietary needs of the people.

Let's not overlook the statement, "God saw all that he had made, and it was very good." What qualifies as "GOOD" to a Holy and Righteous God? Nothing less than absolute perfection! Look around. Is that what you see? Not even close. But aside from overflowing landfills and acid rain there is a bigger problem. US! The way people treat each other, the way we ignore the God who created us. I believe that if we were to work on the latter two issues, the former ones would soon be corrected too. Read on, we will deal with that.

The second chapter of Genesis gives us another view of creation. NOT A SECOND CREATION, as some want to believe. It is a "recap" of the first and only creation. Remember back in verse 27, "male and female he created them." In the next chapter Eve is created separately from Adam.

For the purpose of this study, it will not be necessary to go through every verse as we did with chapter one. The one main point not covered in chapter one of Genesis is the seventh day. In the first three verses of chapter two God says that He "on the seventh day he rested from all his work." Was God tired from all that work? Did God drop into His "Lazy Boy" recliner and take a nap? NO. The more one studies the Bible, the more you will learn that God ALWAYS has a reason for everything that He does. It's just that we can't always understand what His reasons are.

For one thing God was setting precedent of six days of work and one day of rest. Think about it. A day is determined by the rotation of the earth. A month is set, (approximately) by the orbit of the moon around the earth. And a year, of course, is determined by the rotation of the earth around our sun. But where do we get the week? It comes only from the precedent set by God at the time of the creation. God knew that our human bodies would need a time of rest. We also need time which we can spend with our Creator.

God also likes to use "foreshadows." He will use events from the past which relate to events yet in the future. In Isaiah 46:10; He says, "I make known the end from the beginning, from ancient times, what is still to come. I say: My purpose will stand, and I will do all that I please" Does the "precedent" set in the beginning declare "THE END"? We shall revisit this possibility in chapter nine.

Genesis 2:20-22; "So the man gave names to all the livestock, the birds of the air and all the beasts of the field. But for Adam no suitable helper was found. So, the Lord God caused the man to fall into a deep sleep, and while he was sleeping, he took one of the man's ribs and closed up the place with flesh. Then the Lord God made a woman from the rib he had taken out of the man, and he brought her to the man."

Contrary to popular belief, humans did not start out as illiterate cave men. Adam was able to give names to all the animals, fish and birds. He must have been a veritable zoologist.

And NO! Eve was not an afterthought. God has his way of making a point. In this case God let Adam see that there was something lacking. That "special someone" who would share life with him. He had already seen that the other creatures had mates. Where was Adam's?

It is interesting to note that woman came from man, not the other way around. Men have an X and a Y chromosome. Women have two X chromosomes. If man had come from woman, there would have been no source for the Y chromosome. Ponder that for a moment.

The third chapter of Genesis is given the heading, "The Fall of Man." Eve was caused to question the clear admonition of God. "Did God really say, 'You must not eat from any tree in the garden'?" She responds correctly, "We may eat from the trees in the garden, but God did say, 'You must not eat fruit from the tree that is in the middle of the garden, and you must not touch it, or you will die.'"

Here comes the first lie ever told. "You will not surely die." This is one of Satan's favorite tricks. To get a person to question what they know to be true. Then the second lie came, "For God knows that when you eat of it your eyes will be opened, and you will be like God, knowing good and evil."

It was because of this, that the whole world has been cursed. Do you think it unfair since you didn't eat from that tree? You've done just as bad. We all have! Do you think that this caught God off guard? Did the members of the Godhead call a meeting and ask, "What do we do now?" NO! God knew that if He gave man "freewill" there would be big problems. Yet if He had not given man freewill, we would all be puppets, waiting for our strings to be pulled. Before the first man was created, God had a plan ready to bail us out. In fact, the First Timothy 1:8-10 tells us that "This grace was given us in Christ Jesus before the beginning of time."

In the fourth chapter of Genesis, we meet the brothers, Cain and Abel. You will recall that Cain killed his brother Abel. Afterward Cain was afraid that someone would kill him. Genesis 4:15; "But the Lord said to him, 'Not so, if anyone kills Cain, he will suffer vengeance seven times over.' Then the Lord put a mark on Cain so that no one who found him would kill him."

This was the first murder in history. But God had a plan for Cain and protected him. Check Genesis 9:6; "Whoever sheds the blood of man, by man shall his blood be shed; for in the image of God has God made man."

God had a reason to let Cain live.

Genesis 4:17; "Cain lay with his wife, and she became pregnant and gave birth to Enoch." Here comes the part of this study that will blow your mind. Where did Cain get his wife? Think about it! We started with Adam and Eve, just two people, one couple. God never created anyone else. Cain married his sister. He can't do that, you protest. Close relatives are not allowed to marry. Today you would be right, but we are talking about the second generation after creation. Not only were there no other girls to choose from, but there were no "genetic burdens" to affect the offspring.

Today the "gene pool" is loaded with genetic mistakes. The more closely you are related to your spouse, the more likely these mistakes will show up in your children. In the second generation after creation there would have been no genetic mistakes to pass to the next generation. In the twelfth chapter of genesis, we read about Abram who was married to his half-sister, Sarai, their names were later changed to Abraham and Sarah. There was a similar situation after the flood, Genesis 6. Noah had three sons so the next generation would have married first cousins. It was not until later that the law against close relatives marrying was given.

The sixth chapter of Genesis is about the great flood. First of all, I want you to understand that the ark was not some dinky little boat with the necks of giraffes sticking out of the top. It was the largest vessel ever built before the age of steel hulled vessels. It was 450 feet long, 75 feet wide, and 45feet high. Its capacity was greater than 522 stock cars. It's height to width ratio made it virtually impossible to capsize. It had no rudder nor sails as its purpose was only to float. God would see that it landed where He wanted.

Genesis 7:8-9; says, "Pairs of clean and unclean animals, of birds and of all creatures that move along the ground, male and female, came to Noah and entered the ark, as God had commanded Noah." There was no need for Noah and sons to round up the animals.

As mentioned earlier, the forty days and forty nights of rain that fell creating the great flood, possibly was the collapse of a water vapor canopy. In Genesis 7; 11-12 we read; "In the six hundredth year of Noah's life, on the seventeenth day of the second month—on that day all the springs of the great deep burst forth, and the floodgates of heaven were opened. And rain fell on the earth forty days and forty nights."

This would have involved erupting volcanoes and earthquakes. The purpose of this flood was to wipe out every trace of a wicked world. There would have been many changes to the earth in bringing about the flood, and many more at the end of the flood. The earth prior to the flood was much different than now. It had rolling hills, but the mountains were not as we see today. At the end of the flood God deepened the oceans and raised the mountains. Let's look at what the Scripture has to say about this.

Genesis 7:17-22; "For forty days the flood kept coming on the earth, and as the waters increased, they lifted the ark high above the earth. The waters rose and increased greatly on the earth, and the ark floated on the surface of the water. They rose greatly on the earth, and all the high mountains under the entire heavens were covered. The waters rose and covered the mountains to a depth of more than twenty feet. Every living thing that moved on the earth perished— birds, livestock, wild animals, all the creatures that swarm over the earth, and all mankind. Everything on dry land that had the breath of life in its nostrils died."

Chapter 9 of Genesis begins with the statement, "Then God blessed Noah and his sons, saying to them, 'Be fruitful and increase in number and fill the earth.'" I mention this now because the importance of this verse will become clear shortly. Chapter 10 is called "the table of nations." Do you want a verse-by-verse commentary on that? — I thought not. Let's look at chapter 11.

Genesis 11:1-4; "Now the whole world had one language and a common speech. As men moved eastward, they found a plain in Shinar and settled there.

They said to each other, 'Come, let's make bricks and bake them thoroughly.' They used bricks instead of stone, and tar for mortar. Then they said, 'Come, let us build ourselves a city, with a tower that reaches to the heavens, so that we may make a name for ourselves and not be scattered over the face of the whole earth.'"

Did you catch that? In chapter 9 God told them to <u>fill the earth.</u> But these people wanted to stay in one place. Now, you may have been told that the <u>sin</u> of these people was that they wanted to build a tower to heaven. They were smart enough to know that they couldn't do that. It is more likely that they wanted to use the tower for astrology and other pagan worship. One would think that in so short a time after the great flood, these guys would have known better. But they thumbed their noses at God, and He had to break up their party.

Genesis 11:5-9; "But the Lord came down to see the city and the tower that the men were building. The Lord said, 'If as one people speaking the same language, they have begun to do this, then nothing they plan to do will be impossible for them. Come let us go down and confuse their language so they will not understand each other.'

So, the Lord scattered them from there over all the earth, and they stopped building the city. That is why it was called Babel— because there the Lord confused the language of the whole world. From there the Lord scattered them over the face of the whole earth."

While the Bible speaks of tribes and nations, the word race is only applied to a foot race. When the people were scattered, there was a breaking up of the gene pool. Different groups of people would have had various skin colors. Hair, eyes and other features would also very from one group to another. In this way the so-called "races" were begun. The idea that different races "evolved" at different times and that some were "more advanced" than others is totally wrong. Still, it has been the bases of many atrocities, especially since the time of Darwin's theory of evolution.

Let's just take a moment to look at the facts concerning race. There is only one skin color, it's a protein called "melanin." The more of it you have, the darker your skin will be. The only people who don't have this protein are the unfortunate few who suffer from albinism. When we get down to DNA codes, we find that there is more difference within a so-called "race" than there are between them. Genetically, the difference between "races" is about .01% of the 80,000 or so genes. God does not think in monochrome. He creates things of beauty and infinite variety. God only created one race. It's called the human race, and it was designed to offer more beauty and variation than any other creature. Every person on this earth, no matter your skin color, is a descendent of Noah. We are all related no matter what our skin tone or eye shape may be. Many of our differences are cultural rather than genetic.

CHAPTER 4

....

Proof From Geology

G eology is the study of the origin, history, and structure of the
earth. Most often this is assumed to mean not only rocks but
the formation of fossils, the geologic column and mountains,
rivers, lakes and other features of the earth. For the purpose of this study,
I will reserve the discussion of fossils to its own chapter.

Evolutionary geologists claim that the many layers of strata which are
found around the Earth record millions of years of Earth history. Is that a
proven fact? NO! They also claim that radiometric dating methods prove
their long ages theory. Is that a proven fact? NO! The only reason that they
insist on millions of years is that it is known that evolution couldn't happen
in a short time.

Let's debunk that radiometric dating business right up front. First of
all, most people only know a little about Carbon 14. C 14 can only be used
only on organic material, and it has nothing to do with millions of years,
its half- life is only 5730 years, +/- 40. The longest range of age that it can
(supposedly) be used for is from 58,000 to 62,000 years.

Here is how radiometric dating is supposed to work. If you took an
amount of pure uranium-238 which had no lead in it, 4.5 billion years
later one half of it would have turned to lead -206. After nine billion years
¾ of it would be lead. It is the same with other radiometric elements, the
unstable (mother element) decays into the stable (daughter element) and
the process is measured by the "half- life," or time required to change 50%

of the material from the mother to daughter elements. The age is calculated by the ratio of mother to daughter elements contained in the sample.

The methods that are used on rocks are; Uranium/Lead (Ur/ Pb), Potassium/Argon Isochron (K/Ar), or Rubidium/ Strontium Isochron (Rb/ Sr). These are the most common radiometric clocks and there are many others. The question that you should be asking is, "How reliable are those methods?" Most people simply assume that if science says it's true, it must be true. There are many other methods that can be used but the majority of them do not yield the millions or billions of years that evolution requires.

What do you suppose would happen if you were to bring a rock into a science lab and ask to have it dated? First off, they would want to charge you a few thousand dollars for the tests. Then, SURPRISE! They will want to know where the rock came from. Specifically, what strata did it come from and what fossils were in those strata. This information will give them a clue as to how old the rock should be (by evolutionary standards).

The dirty little secret is that they use fossils to date the rocks and rocks to date the fossils. That is circular reasoning. In practice, there are at least three assumptions in any radiometric dating process. 1) That the rate of decay has been the same in the past. 2) The original amount of both the mother and daughter elements are known. 3) That the sample has been in a closed system and no "leaching" in or out of any of the elements has taken place. If any of these assumptions are wrong the entire process is a matter of "garbage in, garbage out." The public is never told of the shenanigans that go on behind the scenes.

When samples are tested by different methods the ages can be greatly different with each method. Cardenas Basalts from the Grand Canyon yielded 715,000,000 years by the K/Ar method and 1.17 billion years by the Rb/Sr method. That's a lot of difference. Moon rocks dated 4.6 to 8.2 billion years by the Ur/Pb method and 2.3 to 3.76 billion years by the K/Ar method. These tests were done on rocks of unknown age. That is, we had no historical record of their age. Let's look at some dates for rocks of known age, formed in historical times.

With an historical date of 3,300 years, a sample from Mt. Rangitoto near Auckland, New Zealand was tested by the K/Ar method and was dated at 485,000 years. We also have well- documented examples from two volcanoes in Hawaii. The known historical dates of these eruptions are 1800 and 1801, yet the dates yielded by K/Ar dating ranged from 140 million to 2.96 billion years. It is not at all uncommon for samples from upper layers to date as being older than samples from farther down. This, of course, is simply not possible. Because these dating methods are notoriously inaccurate, we should not accept them simply because a scientist said that they are right.

Evolutionists won't debate creationists in the public arena. They simply don't want the weakness of their arguments to be known. When thinking people see the evidence side by side the majority will accept the creation viewpoint.

Other "clocks" that indicate younger ages are things like the receding Moon. Tidal friction between the Earth's terrestrial surface and the water moving over it causes energy to be added to the Moon. The result of this is an increase in the distance between the Earth and the Moon. In the early 1980s this recession was measured at four centimeters per year. Physicist Donald De Young says: "One cannot extrapolate the present 4 cm/year separation rate back into history. It has that value today but was more rapid in the past because of tidal effects. In fact, the separation rate depends on the distance to the 6th power, a very strong dependence... the rate... was perhaps 20 m/ year 'long' ago, and the average is 1.2m/year."

This would mean that the age of the Moon must be less than 750 million years, which is only 20% of the 4.5 billion years that evolutionists claim. It is likely much less than 10,000 years old.

Another indication of a young Earth is the fact that oil wells are under pressure. That is a big problem if you want to believe in millions of years. Rocks are porous and the pressure in oil wells would be gone just like a slow leak in a tire. Most of the pressure should be gone in about 10,000 years. What seems to make the most sense is to believe that most of the oil resulted from Noah's flood, about 4,600 years ago. That would put enough raw materials down in a short time to produce our oil; natural gas and coal fields and it would still have plenty of pressure behind it.

Speaking of oil; what is it that we refer to oil as? It's a fossil fuel! We also call coal and natural gas fossil fuels. The most likely reason for all of those fossil fuels being here in great abundance is that they are a result of a cataclysmic event. There is no better explanation of how we could have so much fossil fuel deposited all around the world. Slow, bit by bit processes over long ages just won't get the vast volumes of fuels that we know are there.

Why is the Sun still there? For the last few hundred years scientists have been measuring the Sun and they tell us that it is shrinking at a rate of 5 feet per hour. If this rate has been constant, one million years ago it would have been so close to the Earth that no life could have existed. At 11.2 million years it would have physically been touching the Earth. That surely blows the 4.5 billion years idea of the evolutionists. The rate of shrinkage of the Sun is about 1% of its diameter per thousand years. That is no problem if the Earth is only six thousand years old as the Bible indicates.

As I mentioned at the beginning of this chapter, carbon 14 is not used for rocks; it works with organic samples. We will discuss it more in the next chapter but for now there is a detail that fits the present discussion. C-14 is produced when radiation from the Sun strikes Nitrogen-14 atoms in the upper atmosphere. Because the atmosphere is not yet saturated with C-14 it has not reached equilibrium. The state of equilibrium should be reached in 30,000 years; therefore, the Earth must be younger than that.

The population of the Earth doubles every fifty years. Starting with one couple at only half the current growth rate we would reach the present population in less than 4,000 years. Remember too, it all started over after Noah's flood, 4600 years ago.

Okay, but doesn't the strata accumulate one layer at a time? That's true enough but it is NOT confined to one layer per year. In fact, it often happens that a large number of strata can be laid down in an hour.

Is there anything in modern history that gives us a clue as to how we could get numerous layers of strata in a short time? YES! The eruption of Mt. Saint Helens on May 18, 1980 has told us a great deal about such deposits. This was the most scientifically studied volcanic eruption in history. The scientific community knew that it was going to blow, and they were ready to observe the entire process. But after the eruption they were strangely silent about the findings. When Mt. Saint Helens blew, she blew their theories of long ages of time for the earth's stratification.

Mt. Saint Helens is a small volcano in Washington State. The 1980 eruption leveled 3.2 billion board feet of prime forest, enough to build 640,000 houses. The rockslide displaced the water of Spirit Lake producing waves as much as 850 feet high. The returning waters brought soil and trees into the lake making a deposit 320 feet thick. Do you begin to get the idea that strata isn't laid down a fraction of an inch at a time?

Whenever the subject of geology comes up, I can't help but recall Luke 19:39-40; "some of the Pharisees in the crowd said to Jesus, 'Teacher, rebuke your disciples!' 'I tell you,' he replied, 'if they keep quiet, the stones will cry out.'"

I see in the study of geology that the stones are crying out that this world was created by the all-powerful God, not by chance evolutionary processes. Turn your Bible to the book of Romans, chapter one and read verses 21-25.

"For although they knew God, they neither glorified him as God nor gave thanks to him, but their thinking became futile, and their foolish hearts were darkened. Although they claimed to be wise, they became fools and exchanged the glory of the immortal God for images made to look like mortal man and birds and animals and reptiles."

"Therefore, God gave them over in the sinful desires of their hearts to sexual impurity for the degrading of their bodies with one another. They exchanged the truth of God for a lie and worshiped and served created things rather than the Creator - who is forever praised. Amen."

Read those two paragraphs again, slowly! Think about how well they tell the story of our world today. Think about how your tax dollars can only be used to teach the lie of evolution and turn your children away from the God whom they will face in judgment one day.

DO NOT MISS THIS POINT! It is your responsibility to see that your children know the truth about God and what he requires of them. If you don't set the example by putting God first in your own life your kids are not likely to ever give him serious thought. If you don't make an effort to change the direction that this nation is headed, who will?

Have you read the Old Testament? How many times does it tell of nations that turned away from God and were destroyed because of their willful defiance of God's laws? Don't think for a minute that these United States will escape that same fate! Okay; there I am on my soap box again, but someone needs to wake people up to what is going on before it's too late, if it isn't too late already.

Let's get back to the subject of geology. In the aftermath of the eruption of Mt. St. Helens and subsequent eruptions since then, there have been some amazing discoveries. As stated already, there were many trees dislodged and deposited in Spirit Lake. Over time, and that being only a few years, those trees sank at different times, root end first to the bottom of the lake. This gives us a picture of how the famous "Petrified Forest" came into being. Because of the density of the roots the trees sink root end first thus we have polistrate fossilization if we wait long enough for that to happen.

Before these trees sink, they rub together while floating and the bark peels off and is deposited in the lake Over a few years we end up with what looks like a series of forests, one above the other, at the bottom of the lake. There can be little doubt that the Petrified Forest came about in this way. It was a single forest destroyed by a single event.

We can also see in the aftermath of Mt. St. Helens the beginning of a coal bed on the bottom of Spirit Lake. It is not taking long ages to produce coal as we were taught in school. We can observe nature working in real time. There is no reason to believe that this earth is millions of years old.

Turn your attention to the Grand Canyon. Think! What are we watching happen at Spirit Lake? Is it not likely that this is a scale model of what created the Grand Canyon? If you allow what we can observe happening in our own time guide your thought processes, there is only one logical conclusion. The evidence from geology fits very well with what we read in the Scripture, "In the beginning God created."

In the months following the May 18, 1980, eruption of Mt. St. Helens, there were two more eruptions. That third eruption was a lava flow which turned into a hot mud flow as it crossed the Toutle River. This diverted the river and cut a 17-mile-long series of canyons which ranged up to 140 feet deep. All this was done in just hours.

Major events such as this should have made leading news headlines. Why isn't this in your high school science textbooks? It is all about "keeping the faith." Evolution is nothing more than a "godless religion!" It has nothing to do with observable facts. When the evidence supports Biblical Creation, (as it most often does), it must be censored!

Your public-school textbooks will show you a chart called the "geologic column." It lists the "ages" that are supposed to have occurred by evolutionary reckoning. There is just one little problem with the geologic column; it can only be found in the textbooks! In the real world no more than 20%, at best, of the earth's land surface will have three of the geologic periods in the right order. For those of you who have forgotten the names of those geologic column eras I will list them for you.

In the first group we start with the Archaean era, followed by the Lower, Middle, Upper, and Late Pre-Cambrian eras. These all fall under the Pre- Cambrian Era group. These are very far down and the lowest should have no fossilized life forms in them.

The second group is the Paleozoic Era which consists of the Cambrian, Ordovician, Silurian, Devonian, Mississippian, Pennsylvanian, and Permian eras. In this group we should see the first invertebrate sea life. Then fish, the first land plants and reptiles.

In the Mesozoic group we have the Triassic, Jurassic, and the Cretaceous eras. These groups should have the first dinosaurs, small animals and primitive birds. Modern vegetation now begins to appear.

The fourth and final group is the Cenozoic group made up of the Tertiary, Paleocene, Eocene, Oligocene, Miocene, Pliocene, and the Pleistocene epochs. Next to come are the first primates and flowering plants. Modern mammals, whales and apes appear and finally man.

The biggest problem I had in writing those last four paragraphs is the fact that it's all a fairy tale. NOWHERE in this world do we find these eras in the order that evolutionists claim we should find them. But evolutionists are never caught without an answer. They have a code word for this problem, "Problematica." Don't bother trying to look that up in the dictionary, it's not there. It is just a word that the Paleontologists use to describe out of order fossils. You must understand, the rock layers are dated by the fossils that are found in them.

We will deal more with fossils in chapter six. Let's talk about continental drift. When I speak of Continental drift, I don't mean the time that you slid your daddy's Lincoln off of the road. As I mentioned earlier, there is a puzzle-like fit between the land masses on both sides of the Atlantic Ocean. The rocks and minerals match up very well too. There are also fossil types that match from one side of the Atlantic to the other. What we don't see from the surface is the Mid-Atlantic ridge which sits right smack dab in the middle of the ocean.

Some want to believe that the continents are still drifting slowly apart. There is little to no evidence that this is still happening. Scientists have tried to date the ocean floor at various points to see when the continents drifted apart. Their dating methods show the northern ocean floor to be much younger than the southern ocean floor. That can only be the fault of the dating methods. The questions that we should ask are; when did the continent split apart, why did it split, and how long did that take?

The global flood is the key to understanding geology. When we start with a good knowledge of the Bible and then look at the world around us, the pieces begin to fit together. Scripture tells us that at the end of the flood God raised the mountains and lowered the ocean floors to give the flood waters a place to go. That answers when and the why questions. As to how long it took, I would say, not very long, you can read more about that in the eighth chapter of Genesis. This was a supernatural act of God.

In 1961 Dr. Henry Morris and Dr. John Whitcomb published their book, "The Genesis Flood: the Biblical record and its scientific implications." I highly recommend that book to all who want to understand geology and the truth of the Bible. For more than half of a century this book has been the definitive publication for Biblical creationism.

Frankly friends, those who doubt any part of the Biblical creationism are calling God a liar. It is my purpose to help you find and understand God's Word, His truth, and His will for your life.

This is what you need to know. In the beginning God created the earth and all that was on the earth. He did this in six days, about six thousand years ago. But man, who was intended to be the steward of the world, did not retain God in their minds. They became so wicked that God had to put an end to the society that existed in those days. "But Noah found favor in the eyes of the Lord." (Genesis 6:8).

It took Noah one hundred and twenty years to build the ark. During that time, he was warning those around him that there was to be a flood.

But they wouldn't listen to him. "Noah, you're nuts! There aren't any lakes around here, and what the *#@ is a flood anyway? What do you mean, rain?" You see, the Scripture tells us that the earth was watered by a mist, it had never rained before. No one took Noah seriously, so it was just Noah and his three sons and their wives who were saved and reestablished the human race on the earth.

Not only did it rain for forty days and nights but "the springs of the great deep burst forth, and the floodgates of the heavens were opened." (Genesis 7:11). The water covered the highest mountains by twenty feet. Skeptics claim that there isn't enough water to reach that depth. They also look at Mars which has no liquid water and say that Mars once had a global flood. The earth is 70% covered by water and if you could smooth out the surface to make it round as a ball the water would be about two miles deep.

The flood was God's judgment on a world that had turned its back on their creator. Look around, they were just like us. The more liberal our society becomes, the more ungodly it will be. I don't mean to offend my many liberal friends but that is a fact of life. Liberalism always pushes God out of their way. That has been true everywhere that liberalism has taken over a government.

Okay, so the world was covered by water. Where did all of that water go? It's still here. It's in our oceans, some of it is in icebergs, some in the atmosphere, but it's all still here. God had to make the oceans deeper to dry the land. This is probably when the continents were separated. In the process we ended up with things like the Grand Canyon and deep layers of stratified rock and soil. All of the plants and animals that had lived before the flood became ether fossils or fossil fuels.

What more do you need to know? You need to know God, personally! That is the reason I am writing this book. I want to help you get to know your creator in a personal way. He wants that too.

CHAPTER 5

....

Proof From Biology

W hich came first, the chicken or the egg? Ask someone who has had experience with chickens; like me. It obviously had to be the chicken. Not only that, but there had to be a rooster too. Now, if you don't know why there had to be a rooster you had best ask your mommy. The egg by itself would never become a chicken as it must be sat on by the hen for three weeks before it hatches, Furthermore, the hen must go out in the grass in the morning while there is due to wet her feathers, then go back and sit on the eggs again. She must also turn the eggs over every day. My point is this; life doesn't just happen. There are many ancillary things which must happen that are not obvious to the uninformed (evolutionists).

One morning I sat down at the computer and went online. One of the news items that were running on AOL said, "Appendix May Be Useful Organ After All." I knew that at least twenty years ago. But then, these guys are caught up in the "religion" of evolution. That is why they are so far behind in discovering what these organs are for. In the 1890s there were 180 "vestigial organs." They were believed to be useless leftovers from our evolutionary past. Today the purpose of all of them is known.

The so-called "tail bone" was one of those vestigial organs. Yet we now know that it is absolutely necessary. It is the attachment point for muscles in that region.

"Gill slits" are another example of the vestigial organ myth. This is found in nearly every high school science book and is proclaimed at abortion clinics. But there is just one little problem, there is never a time when a fetus has "gills." Nor are there any "slits." Maybe it's not right to call them "gill slits." The fact is that we know that they will become the tonsils, thymus, and parathyroid glands, all important parts of your immune system.

And a fetus is <u>NOT</u> just a blob of tissue. Any Doctor worthy of his/her degree knows that you can determine who its parents are, (or would be). A woman who wants a child would refer to her fetus as her <u>baby</u> from the very moment she knows that she has conceived. I will state for the record that I would not tell a woman who had been raped that she could not decide for herself if she should have an abortion. It is those who profit from abortions who use rape as their "foot in the door" to allow abortion for convenience to be legal.

If you want to see a real miracle, get the video, "Fearfully and Wonderfully Made." In just over an hour, you will see at least eighteen miracles. All the way from conception, implantation, growth, and birth, the process of bringing a child into this world is a series of miracles. What would seem to be insurmountable obstacles are overcome in mind-boggling ways.

Do you realize that fertilization should be impossible? The sperm is not from the same body as the ovum; therefore, it should be rejected by the ovum. (Remember, organ donors have to be matched to recipients and still, the recipient will need anti- rejection drugs). Likewise, implantation should also be impossible. Again, this is a foreign cell and should not be accepted and allowed to implant.

Now to those who want to say, "Our bodies, our rights." <u>IT'S NOT YOUR BODY!</u> It is a separate, unique individual. The fetus is usually of a different blood type, half the time of a different sex and unlikely to be a tissue match to its mother. There is a "miraculous" system by which the blood of the mother transfers oxygen and nutrients to the baby across a barrier which allows the two individuals to have different blood types.

After going through a long series of miracles we arrive at the moment of birth only to discover, like the guy who built a boat in his basement, it's too big to go through the door. Yes, soft tissue stretches, (painfully, so women tell me) but it's not soft tissue that I'm referring to. Do you know what a pelvis looks like? You see the baby has to go through that little opening at the bottom of the pelvis. There is just no way that this can happen, except for another miracle. There are three joints in the pelvis designed by the Creator God. These joints soften and allow the pelvis to open just a little bit so that when the baby's head is turned, like a key in a lock, it just fits through.

After at least eighteen such miracles, are you willing to tell me that it all just happened by chance? Clearly, there had to be an infinite intelligence behind the entire process of reproduction. The evolutionary idea of solving one problem at a time would have caused the species to become extinct in the first generation.

Have you ever wondered why any species would reproduce by sexual means in the first place? That means that the first of any species must find a mate of the opposite sex or the species will die out.

So, what is evolution anyway? There are actually two types of evolution. One happens every day, the other has never been observed. These two types are "microevolution" and "macroevolution."

Microevolution is an unfortunate term because it implies evolution. Microevolution refers to small mistakes in DNA copying. IT DOES NOT involve increasing complexity or new information as required for evolution. There is also genetic variation but again, there is no new information and no new species. We only see random variation within a kind.

Macroevolution: it has never been observed. With the discovery of the DNA / RNA genetic code it is obvious that macroevolution is impossible. Any mistake in the copying of the DNA code will be a mutation, not a step upward in the evolutionary process. The belief that extrapolating small, random changes, over long periods of time can create a new species is not supported by observation, experiments, or the fossil record.

Evolution is a theory that the facts have failed.

What about the "Miller experiment?" I'm sure that you have seen Stanley Miller's experiment in textbooks from middle school on up. In the early 1950's Miller set up some lab equipment and put in the type of gases that he believed were in the atmosphere of the early earth. After zapping his concoction with an electric spark, he was able to get some amino acids from the device. Did he really create life in a test tube? No, far from it!

The theory of evolution requires that life come about by random chance. Miller used "intelligence." Miller used a closed system. Miller used the wrong gases. Miller got the wrong results.

It is now known that the gases that were used in the Miller experiment were not the same as would have been available in the supposed early earth atmosphere. Worse still is the fact that he collected both left- and right-hand amino acids. In life, ALL amino acids in life are left-handed. Adding right-handed amino acids will poison the mix. Today, even Stanley Miller admits that his experiment was a failure.

I'm not throwing stones at Dr. Miller. He only did what seemed to be the right thing to do given the understanding of science at the time. Like all who have been raised in an educational system that claims evolution to be fact, his understanding was flawed by wrong teaching.

Just in case this hasn't been complicated enough for you I'll throw in the fact that there are over 2,000 types of amino acids. Of these only 20 are commonly found in biological proteins. Life therefore must be very selective.

What else could be wrong with Miller's experiment? First of all, the atmosphere, the presence of oxygen prevents amino acids from forming. Yet without oxygen the amino acids would be destroyed by the ultraviolet rays from the sun. Secondly; amino acids could not have formed in water due to hydrolysis; the action of water decomposing molecules. Third; Miller's experiment used intelligent design from start to finish. Forth; Miller produced a mixture of left and right handed amino acids which are not used in life. When something dies the amino acids revert to a 50/50 mixture of left and right-handed ones. Fifth; the natural tendency is always toward a 50/50 mixture of left and right-handed amino acids.

Despite the fact that Miller's experiment failed to produce organic compounds used in life, many textbooks continue to use it to support evolution.

DNA is the blueprint for a living being. It controls the growth of a fetus causing the different organs and appendages to form in just the right places. The complexity of the process is still not fully understood.

When I was in middle school, (in a previous millennium), we were taught about cell division. One cell becomes two cells. Then they become four cells, then eight cells. Whoa! That would be like yeast bread rising in a pan. Every cell would be a carbon copy of the one before it. In a living creature there are many different types of cells, and they must all work together in intricate ways.

There is yet another type of DNA known as Mitochondrial DNA. It was first believed to be passed only from the mother but that is now in question. In 1989 a group of scientists compared the Mitochondrial DNA of different races and found that all people trace back to a single mother who lived about 100,000 – 200,000 years ago. They referred to her as "Eve." After measuring the rate of Mitochondrial DNA mutations, it was found that the rate of change was 20 times faster than previously believed. That means that "Eve" lived only 5,000 to 10,000 years ago. With this new, younger age for Eve being so close to the Biblical timeline the story never made the news.

Another discovery that didn't make the headlines is the unfossilized dinosaur bones found on the North Slope of Alaska. There are thousands of them, and they show very little permineralization. In other words, they are not fossils but fresh bones.

It had been predicted that DNA could not last much more than 10,000 years. Then someone discovered a green magnolia leaf in strata that was dated at 17 million years old. Its DNA was a match to modern magnolia leaves. Once again, the facts don't fit the theory. As a Biblical creationist it seems obvious that the leaf is not 17 million years old.

Why haven't you read of these things in your local paper or seen it on the news? Few scientists are willing to "go against the flow" so far as the "accepted doctrine" is concerned. If they want to get funding for their work, or to stay employed, they won't publish facts that don't fit the evolutionary belief system. Just ask Dr. Mary Schweitzer, formerly of the Montana State University. In 1990 she found some T. Rex bones which contained dried blood cells. Had these bones been 65 million years old the blood cells should have been long gone. Dr. Schweitzer published her findings in "Earth" magazine in 1996. Because Mary had published her findings in the popular press she was "run out of town on a rail." She is now at North Carolina State University.

The oldest living thing on Earth is either an Irish Oak or a Bristlecone pine. These are between 4,500 and 4,770 years old. Since these trees are still alive it suggests that something happened about that many years ago to destroy all the older trees. Noah's flood is estimated to have been 4,600 years ago.

The belief that man descended from apes has once again made monkeys out of evolutionists. This is due to the discovery of four genes which are located in three separate regions of chromosome 1.1 and play an important role in the development of the brain. These genes are named: SRGAP2A, SRGAP2B, SRGAP2C and SRGAP2D. Of these four genes, three (B, C, and D) are not found in any other mammal, including the apes.

Evolutionists want to claim that the SRGAP gene was inherited from an "ape-like ancestor" and that it somehow moved to different parts of the chromosome. This is not at all a likely scenario as this gene is found in the "centromere", a specialized part of the chromosome which is a very stable area. Once more the evolutionists are left struggling for answers to explain away the obvious, "In the beginning, God created."

Using a biological paradigm known as independent lineage sorting humans have been linked to gorilla DNA or chimpanzee DNA depending on which DNA segments you are analyzing. There is no clear path of common ancestry between humans and any other primate. One should expect there to be common design because all primates were designed by the same creator.

Red blood cells were discovered in the body of "Otzi the Ice man", a world-famous frozen natural mummy. Forensic researchers found particles of Otzi's last meal, (deer and bread), and say that his boots appear to be professionally made. An arrowhead was in his shoulder and likely was the cause of death; maybe we should call the homicide squad.

When what appeared to be red blood cells were tested using two techniques, Atomic force microscopy and Raman spectroscopy. Both tests confirm that these were indeed red blood cells. The cells are believed to be 5300 years old, yet these are not the oldest red blood cells to be discovered in un-fossilized remains. The point is that true science does not confirm the millions of years that evolution requires.

Still another question must be resolved. How did biological life forms get here in the first place? In the past evolutionary scientists have simply assumed that life forms could evolve on many planets throughout the universe. But life is too complex; it requires far too many exacting criteria to be found just anywhere. Enter the realm of "Rare Earth."

In 2000 geologist / paleontologist Peter Ward and astronomer / astrobiologist Donald Brownlee published; "Rare Earth: Why Complex Life Is Uncommon in the Universe". Their book details the improbable combination of astrophysical and geological events and circumstances required to bring about complex multicellular life.

To have life as we know it here on the earth you must have oxygen. At sea level our atmosphere contains 21% oxygen, that's just the right amount. You have major problems if there is too little or too much oxygen. Life also requires liquid water. To have liquid water you need the right temperature range. To have the right temperature range you need to have the right heat source and several other factors.

In our case the heat source is the Sun. It just happens to be the right type of star; a G2 dwarf, and is just the right distance away, 93,000,000 miles. Again; too close it would be too hot, too far away would be too cold. Yet even as important as our Sun is we still need something more. We must also have a stabilizing factor; we need a moon at just the right distance and the right size to keep us at a 23.5 degree tilt on our axis. This makes possible our seasons, creates the tides which keep the ocean waters circulating. This also has a temperature stabilizing effect.

Our planet must also be in the "galactic habitable zone" of our solar system. We need a liquid iron core to produce the magnetic field which is a defensive barrier.

Gravity must be just right too. Too little and our atmosphere (air) would be lost, too much and we would be crushed.

As in real estate, location, location, location is the all-important factor. We happen to be not only in the habitable zone, but we are between the spiral arms within the galaxy. This makes it possible to see far out into space and observe the universe. The oxygen rich atmosphere gives us a transparent window to facilitate the observation of things in space.

You may have noticed that these last few factors are not biological. Congratulations! You are very observant. But you must realize that without these factors being exactly right, you could not possibly have biological life. We are told that evolution is a fact even though it has never been observed and there is no scientific explanation of how complex information-bearing molecules could come from nonlife.

The variations that occur in animal and plant life are NOT onward upward evolution but only a reshuffling of the existing "gene pool." Statistically, a protein molecule which consists of thousands of amino acids and having complex genetic machinery all functioning interdependently could never come about by chance random processes.

2 Peter 3:3-7: "First of all, you must understand that in the last days scoffers will come, scoffing and following their own evil desires. They will say, 'Where is this 'coming' he promised? Ever since our fathers died, everything goes on as it has since the beginning of creation.' But they deliberately forget that long ago by God's word the heavens existed and the earth was formed out of water and by water. By these waters also the world of that time was deluged and destroyed. By the same word the present heavens and earth are reserved for fire, being kept for the day of judgment and destruction of ungodly men."

Did you get that? In the last days people will scoff at the idea of creation. They will deliberately forget that God judged the world once before and destroyed it. And they will not believe that He will do so again. This is no time to be unsure of your salvation.

Studies show that the rate of genetic disorders in humans is increasing exponentially. This is not evolving to a higher form but just the opposite. What we should understand from this fact is that the species has not been around for tens of thousands of years. The evidence points to "devolution," not evolution. The second law of thermodynamics tells us that everything is running down and there are no exceptions to that law. While evolutionists insist on long ages of time, in truth time is not on their side.

In his book, "Origin of Species," Charles Darwin claimed that Natural Selection was the mechanism which allowed simple organisms to evolve gradually into the plants and animal we see today. But Natural Selection

49

is a conservative process. Darwin believed that mutations would help the process along, but beneficial mutations have never been observed.

Want to dig a little deeper? Enter the world of Molecular Biology. It was much easier to believe in evolution when we thought of a cell as being like a piece of Jell-O, just a blob of protoplasm. Over the past few decades, we have developed more powerful microscopes which reveal the incredible complexity of what we thought were "simple cells." Not only are the cells not simple but contain highly complex biological machines. Discoveries of science are making the theory of evolution less defensible as time goes on.

In 1986 Michael Denton published his book, "Evolution: A Theory in Crisis." Many Creationist (like me) quickly bought and studied that book. Dr. Denton, an M.D., Ph. D. molecular biologist, explains in detail that "Evolution is still a theory, based on fossils that have never been found, and genetics that have never been observed."

To help you get "the big picture" I will quote in part from a paper written by Steve Hall.

"Minimum Requirements for Self-Reproducing Cell"

"In the days when the theory of evolution was first proposed, it was assumed that there were certain molecules that had the characteristics necessary for reproducing themselves. The belief was that, over millions and millions of years, chance combinations of atoms reached a point where one of these molecules could suddenly reproduce itself. Thus began the simplest forms of "life." Gradually, more atoms were added, the molecules got more complex, multi- celled organisms developed, etc."

"It is now known that there is no molecule that can reproduce itself without the involvement of many other critical molecules. Many have mistakenly believed that DNA molecules replicate themselves. They cannot. A biochemist named Harold Morowitz has tried to make an intelligent guess at how simple a cell could be, and still be able to reproduce itself. He has hypothesized that it might be conceivable for a cell to be able to reproduce itself with as few as one hundred protein molecules, all doing their respective functions (e.g. providing a cell membrane; synthesizing fats; providing energy; synthesizing the building blocks of DNA- the nucleotides; and synthesizing proteins). The cell would need a few messenger RNA molecules, ribosomes, enzymes, and, of course, a DNA molecule."

"There is no way for scientists to conceive of a cell reproducing itself with less complexity. These are the bare minimum requirements. In fact, no known cell reaches this degree of simplicity, but this hypothetical cell represents the bare minimum of "ingredients" that could conceivably be self-reproducing." Copyright 2000 Steve Hall, (steve@aboundingjoy.com) quoted by permission.

I hope that Steve didn't lose you with that study in Molecular Biology. What I want you to see is that life just couldn't happen by chance. The theory of evolution is nothing more than a godless religion, a faith that the facts have failed.

Carbon 14 is used to date biological remains. So, how does it work? C-14 is an unstable radioactive isotope of carbon-12. It is assumed that the ratio of C-12 and C-14 are the same until a plant or animal dies. The C-14 will decay from that time on and the ratio of C-12 to C-14 can then be used to calculate the age of the organic item to be tested. The accuracy of this method relies on faulty assumptions. Tests have shown that the rate of C-14 decay are not constant.

To make C-14 dating work it was assumed that C12 and C-14 were in balance. If there were little to no C-14 at the time of creation it should take over 50,000 years for equilibrium to be reached. Scientists believed that the earth was much older than that, so it was assumed that equilibrium had been reached. The ratio is only 78% of what it should be if the earth were as old as evolutionists want to say that it is.

In actual use C-14 has been used to date a living mollusk as having died 2,000 years ago. Oops, there must be a problem with that dating method. When radiocarbon dates don't yield the desired age that the scientist hope for, they allege "cross-contamination" of the sample. Results that don't affirm the required age are thrown out, but you aren't supposed to know that. The accuracy of C-14 dating relies on faulty assumptions and is subject to human bias.

I will close this chapter with what I have long considered to be the most obvious proof that evolution doesn't work in the way that we are assured that it does. If evolution were true, mothers should have more than two arms.

....

CHAPTER 6

Proof From the Fossil Record

When Charles Darwin set sail on the HMS Beagle in 1831 there was little known about the fossil record. As he wrote "The Origin of Species," (published in 1859), Darwin felt that the fossil record would eventually substantiate his theory. But going on two centuries later the fossils have actually discredited Darwin's theory of evolution.

If evolution were true, there should be numerous transitional fossils in every branch of the evolutionary tree. They just aren't there. Even the few that evolutionists have tried to claim don't stand the test of rational thinking and investigation. And again, there are too few of them. What the fossil record does show is an explosion of many thousands of life forms, all fully formed, followed by catastrophic extinction of many of the species.

Before we get into the fossil record too deeply, I'd like to mention a word that sets an evolutionist's teeth on edge. POLISTRATE FOSSIL! What's wrong with that word? If the evolutionary timeline and the geologic column are what they are said to be; polistrate fossils can't exist.

A polistrate fossil is one that stands on end through many layers of strata. These are found in abundance, all around the world, yet they shouldn't exist. WHY? Because it is supposed to take long periods of time for all those layers of strata to build up. That would mean that these fossils should have decomposed during the process. The only way that polistrate fossils can exist is if the strata were all laid down in a short time. This, of course, does not fit the evolutionary time scale. As so often happens, the facts don't fit the evolutionary story.

How would a Biblical Creationist interpret these polistrate fossils? The Bible tells us of a great flood that was intended to erase the world as it had been, (see Genesis chapter 6). What would you expect to find if this were true? As Ken Hamm likes to say, "Billions of dead things (fossils) buried in rock layers, laid down by water all over the earth." (Ken Hamm is founder of Answers in Genesis). That flood would account for many layers of strata being laid down in a short time. This would allow for such things as polistrate fossils. It would explain why the fossil record appears as an explosion of different kinds of animals, all fully formed, and followed by catastrophic extinction. What we find all over the world in the fossil record fits exactly with what we read in Genesis.

Skeptics like to claim that the waters of "Noah's flood" could not have covered the entire earth. They say that it could only have been a local flood. A local flood would not have killed all of the people and animals because they would have been able to just go to higher ground. Isn't that what people do today when there is a flood? Those skeptics can't explain why there are fossilized sea creatures at the tops of all of our highest mountains. Either those mountains were down below sea level, or the water was up above the mountains.

Let's be sure that we understand what a fossil is made of. I'm sure that you know that dead things decay. If an animal is left lying on the ground it will be scavenged by other animals and birds. There will be little left for the worms to finish. A dead animal or plant must be buried quickly under mud or similar covering. As the decay process begins, organic cells are replaced with inorganic minerals. Therefore, fossils are stone replicas of once living animals or plants.

The majority of fossils are of sea creatures. That's not surprising since they are much more likely to get buried during a catastrophe, like Noah's flood. The most popular fossils are those of dinosaurs. At one time the number of dinosaur types was over one hundred. Fifty or so would be a more accurate number. You see, we usually only find parts of the fossilized creature. Often dinosaurs of the same type would be called by another name simply because it wasn't the same size as one found earlier. And poor

Brontosaurs, the great thunder lizard had to be removed from the books when it was discovered that his family already had the name, Apatosaurus.

A popular evolutionary story is the "horse series." This series will show five different animals with the claim that this is the progression from the four toed "Eohippus" through the three toed Oligocene and Miocene and on to the single toed Pliocene and finally the Pleistocene (modern horse).

What the evolutionists can't explain is by what mechanism did these creatures go from 18 pairs of ribs to 19, then back to 18? If the supposedly 50,000,000-year-old Eohippus was an early horse, why does it still exist in Africa, where it is known as a rock badger?

Evolutionists can't explain why a three toed horse was found in the same stratum as a one toed horse in Oregon. Even worse, a one toed horse was found under a three toed horse in South America. This simply shouldn't be possible. That is, unless you are willing to accept the Genesis flood as being true history.

Fact: a complete "horse series" has never been found in the correct order anywhere in the world. Modern horse fossils have been found in the same strata as the earliest supposed horse fossils.

It should also be noted that the progression from multi-toed to single toed is contradictory to the evolutionary idea that the simple will become more complex. As with all other creatures, there are no transitional forms between the assumed stages of horse development. Each (so called) horse appears abruptly, fully formed and unique. As we find time after time again, evolution is a theory that the facts have failed.

What about those cave men that our educational system assures us are a part of our family tree? Let me tell you some facts that are never included in your textbooks.

Nebraska Man was "created" from a single tooth. Within five years of his discovery, it was found that the tooth was actually from a wild pig. Why doesn't the average high school student know that? Indoctrination!

Neanderthal man, this guy had a larger brain than you do. He walked upright and believed in the supernatural. They buried their dead. Dress him in modern clothes and he would look like your next-door neighbor.

For forty years Piltdown man fooled the world. It was Charles Dawson who found part of a skull and a broken lower jawbone. Sir Arthur Smith Woodward, who was with the British Museum and a priest, Father Teilhard de Chardin joined Dawson. They told of the unusual finds that they had made at Piltdown in the early 1900s.

The jawbone was very ape-like but the teeth had been worn down in the way that human teeth wear down. The canine tooth was missing from the jawbone. Of all the scientists who examined the evidence, only one questioned whether the skull and jawbone belonged together.

When skeptics insisted that they should be allowed to re-examine the Piltdown artifacts they first lowered its age from five hundred thousand years to only fifty thousand years. After further testing it was found that the skull was of a modern human, but the jaw was that of an ape. It was also found that the teeth had been filed down and the jaw was stained with chemicals so that it would appear to be older. Piltdown man was a hoax.

In 1891 Dr. Eugene Dubois went to Java in search of the "missing link." He found a few teeth, a part of a skull and a thigh bone. The thigh bone was found 50 feet from the skull cap. Frankly, there is no reason to believe that the owners of those bones had even seen each other in their life, let alone that they could belong to the same individual. Dr. Dubois failed to tell anyone that he had also found two human skulls in the same stratum as the skull cap. It was more than thirty years before Dubois disclosed the human skulls. One biologist said, "The success of Darwinism was accompanied by a decline in scientific integrity."

"Sinathropus Pekinesis" better known as "Peking Man" was the invention of Dr. Davidson Black of Canada who believed that man began life in China. In 1928 Dr. Black took charge of an excavation near a hill at Peking, China. Father Teilhard de Chardin, whom you read about earlier, was an unofficial observer. He reported the find of a skull which was like the great apes. Dr. Black reported that a skull cap had been found. It was two years later that he finished the model which some say did not comply with the guidelines for constructing such models.

Two large piles of ashes were uncovered which contained many animal bones. The ashes contained many monkey skulls which Black claimed were more of the Peking men. The ash heap that was being excavated was one hundred yards long, eighty feet wide and about twenty feet high. These had been industrial furnaces, probably used when building the ancient city which was where Peking is now. The bones found in the ashes are likely left from the lunch of the workers.

Do not miss this point! While Dr. Black was looking for ape- men, what he found was the remains of an industrial society. These had been intelligent people.

No one knows what became of the fossil bones of Peking Man. Apparently, after the war they were put on an American ship but that is the last we know of them. It has been said that Dr. Pei continued his study of the fossils during the Japanese occupation. It is possible that he felt it wise to destroy those fossils According to Father Patrick O'Connell; "The skulls were, therefore, destroyed before the Chinese government returned to Peking in order to remove the evidence of fraud on a large scale.

I suppose that no discussion of fossils would be complete without the mention of Lucy. She was discovered in Ethiopia by Donald Johanson in 1974. Lucy would have been about 3'6" tall and supposedly was 3.2 million years old. Lucy's skull was gorilla- like with about ¼ the brain size of humans. Her jaw and teeth were gorilla-like, not human. The fingers were long and curved and the toes were the same. Lucy was built to swing from trees; she was in no way human. Others who have studied these remains, Richard Leakey among them, have concluded that two or three species were combined to become Lucy.

Lucy remains in most textbooks in spite of the fact that more and more scientists are rejecting her as a link to humans. As always, truth takes a back seat to the religion of evolution. They will never allow a Devine foot in the door.

A major tenant of evolution is the belief that giant mammals did not coexist with humans. Here again the facts don't fit the evolutionary story. Along Florida's East coast the remains of mastodons, mammoths, and giant ground sloths have been found along with human fossils. At the time these were found researchers claimed that the human fossils had washed in long after the other fossils had been deposited. That idea defies all logic as well as the known principles of fossilization. Then again, evolution isn't based on logic. It is a "godless religion."

Not only giant mammals but giant plants are found in the fossil record. If we take the Bible literally giants are expected. Prior to the flood the environment was much different than it is today. We find dragon flies with eighteen-inch wing spans. That is five times the size of those I've seen here in Ohio's Miami Valley. Not all, but some dinosaurs grew to be very large. What do you think those giants were here for? In a world where plants grew to be very large there was a need for giant lawn mowers. After the flood they were no longer needed as the plants didn't grow to those huge sizes anymore.

The supposed earliest Americans were the Clovis people who lived in caves in New Mexico. There have been "pre-Clovis" fossils found in Tennessee and Texas as well as those mentioned in Florida.

In addition to dinosaurs, fish and other "bone replica" fossils there are fossil fuels. Coal, crude oil and natural gas are a gift from a benevolent God who even while destroying a wicked world, left us with enough fuel to last until the end of time. How do I know that? I've read the book, the one that the creator dictated. Therefore, I know where the fossil fuels came from, and I also know that we are getting very close to the end. God's Word makes it very clear that we cannot know the date of the end, but we are also told to "WATCH" for those signs that lead to the end. I will explain more about that in chapter nine.

Much of what you have been told about the problems with fossil fuels is BUNK. Most of the pollution can be controlled. Still politicians find that they can use a little pseudo-science to their advantage. They can buy the votes of the uninformed and control the activities of business and citizens.

In truth, fossil fuels have made it possible to reach standards of living that were previously unattainable. Most of the electrical power in these United States is generated by coal-fired power plants. As I mentioned earlier, your plug-in electric car will probably have a coal-fired power plant at the other end of the wire. About 1/5th of our power comes from natural gas-powered generators. Those nasty old coal powered plants make it possible for you to live in a comfortable home no matter what the weather; hot or cold just set the thermostat as you please. Whatever you want to do, watch a little TV, work at the computer, or just listen to some music, coal makes it possible.

Petroleum not only greases the gears of industry, it powers nearly every mode of transportation. Technology is getting better at making both gasoline and diesel fuel powered vehicles run cleaner and more efficiently. The search for new ways to power our modern way of life should continue, but not be forced on us without sound logical forethought. What do I mean by that statement? It hasn't helped to give billions to "green" companies which had already been found to be unviable. Well; I guess it helped a few liberal politicians and their cronies who lined their pockets before those companies went bankrupt.

Thirty or so years ago there were a number of wind generators built in this region. Many of them were soon abandon as impractical. Some have installed solar panels; those done in recent years have had some success, but it is still far too expensive for most households. We should keep trying to perfect solar power but let's not burden the taxpayers with the development costs. I am confident that solar power can be made much more cost effective than it is today. Let's go for it!

It would be good to do a little review before we move into the next topics of this book. In chapter one it was established that the liberal educational system has removed God and His morality from public view. The result of banning God from public schools has been devastating. The rules that our Creator has set forth are not to limit our enjoyment but to protect us and ensure our happiness. If we are to get our nation; or even just our own lives on track, we must strive to be right with God.

I must say that some of my friends consider themselves to be liberals. Please know that I care about those people deeply. I also don't think that they are as liberal as they think that they are. Why do I say that? I know that these friends are very, very generous when they learn of the needs of others. STATISTCAL FACT: Christians and conservatives are much more generous than liberals where charitable donations are concerned. I recall a presidential election a few years ago. When the liberal candidate disclosed his tax records I was stunned. This guy with all of his multiple millions had given less to charity than I do.

In the second chapter we discussed how prophecy proves that the Bible was dictated by the Creator God. Only a being who was outside of time could know in infinite detail what was to take place in centuries to come. Bible prophecy is the atheist's nightmare.

Chapter three was a verse-by-verse explanation of Genesis chapter one and other verses that pertain to the subject of creation. That included the great flood and the reason that God created a language barrier and caused the gene pool to be split. That was the beginning of what we call "races."

You have read in the fourth chapter how geology fits what you would expect to find as a young earth creationist. The book of Genesis tells us what we should expect to find when we take an honest look at the geological record. That record does not fit at all with the evolutionary story. Remember: evolution is a faith that the facts have failed.

The fifth chapter dealt with the biological evidence and how it fits creation much better than evolution. Nowhere do we find complex information systems coming about by chance random processes. Information always comes from a greater intelligence. The second law of thermodynamics, for which there are no exceptions, tells us that everything runs down. Everything wears out, grows old, and becomes disorganized. No one has ever observed upward evolution of anything.

In this, the sixth chapter we have seen that the fossils, which Darwin hoped would confirm his theory, has actually refuted the theory of evolution. Rather than a progression from simple to complex life forms we see an explosion of all types of life followed by catastrophic extinction. Real scientific facts do not fit the theory of evolution. The fossil record fits much better with the Genesis account of creation, followed by a global flood.

CHAPTER 7

....

So, What's the Verdict

S ince the preponderance of evidence is on the side of creation, why is evolution "the only game in town" so far as schools are concerned? It hasn't always been that way, but over time those who don't want to go by the rules that God has set forth have taken over. They run the educational system, the government, and the news media. Education is no longer about learning how to think, but what to think. It has become indoctrination.

Sir Julian Huxley, grandson of Thomas Huxley who was known as "Darwin's bulldog" was asked, "Why do you think that evolution caught on so quickly?" "[I suppose the reason] we all jumped at the Origin [Origin of Species] was because the idea of God interfered with our sexual mores." While this reasoning fits with many other laws of God that they don't like, let's examine what "sexual freedom" has gotten us.

If you go to a grocery store and want to get a good apple you can pick one up and look it over, but you can't take a bite out of it and put it back. Having sex outside of marriage is like taking a bite out of the apple before committing to it (buying it), leaving it for the next person. Having sex without marriage is to have sex with someone else's future spouse. That may not seem like a big deal if you're only thinking of the physical part of it. But one cannot escape the spiritual aspect of the sexual union.

Hang on while I put my counselors cap on, (I am a certified Christian counselor). God created sex, and He intended it to be for a lifetime union. By God's design our world functions with both natural and spiritual laws.

It should not then be surprising that having sex creates an eternal, spiritual bond. In godly relationships this knitting together of two souls can be a great blessing. Ungodly unions, however, can be very destructive; this is the reason why so many have intimacy issues. They have scattered parts of their spiritual being all over. This is a drain on their spiritual power and leaves them unable to trust others and even themselves.

This problem can and must be corrected if one is to have an intimate, trusting relationship with another person. I have known some who have developed some very good business relationships only to have them fall apart when that relationship grew to be too personal. I will explain later how to find relief from this problem. You may need a professional Christian counselor who can lead you out of this difficult situation. Usually this can be done in a few sessions. However, the complete healing from wrong soul ties can take months and it can be emotionally painful.

So, what else has "sexual freedom" brought to our society? It has brought us an increase in sexually transmitted diseases. One out of four girls in the 15 to 25 age group have venereal warts. Transmission is not prevented by condoms, and this is a pre-cursor to cervical cancer. It has been said that "Young people have become rats in a failed social experiment."

The pill, diaphragms, condoms and abortion, these all encourage young people to engage in risky behavior. They believe that they can have sex without consequences. They are wrong! The infections that are passed sexually can be life altering, if not life ending. Thirty percent of sexually transmitted diseases are incurable. Although condom packages say they are 95% effective at stopping pregnancy, real world studies show that couples having regular sex with condoms stand a 16% chance of pregnancy in any given year. Would you board a plane that only had an 84% chance of reaching its destination?

One more item that you'll never hear about from Planned Parenthood is that women who have abortions have an increased risk of breast cancer. That is because they push condoms and condoms fail, increasing the demand for their most lucrative "service" – abortion. It's big money for them, and they don't care how many lives are ruined in the process. Sexual freedom is the freedom to ruin your life and that of others too.

The greatest concern of most girls after having sex is that they might get pregnant. In truth, the odds of contracting an STD are four times as high as that of conceiving. Want to know more? Go to pamstenzer.com for some real eye opening, if not heart-breaking information about teen sex.

The pill is a steroid, as are injected and patch hormonal contraceptives, they cause depression, lower libido, make women more irritable, (like having continual P.M.S.), and cause weight gain. They cause the body to think that it is in the first few weeks of pregnancy.

About half of all women quit taking the pill because of the side effects. I would be remiss to neglect telling you of one other side effect of the pill. It contains not just one but two carcinogens. Don't miss that! The pill contains two (2) cancer causing hormones. It doesn't make sense to take a daily dose of carcinogens.

Abortion raises the odds of breast cancer, and the pill also raises the odds of breast cancer. Just as in that old margarine commercial, "It's not nice to fool Mother Nature."

While researching this material I discovered that there are four types of breast tissue "lobules." These are surrounded by supportive and connective tissue. At birth you have type 1 lobules which are very immature. These will develop into type 2 lobules at puberty. Both type 1 and type 2 lobules are susceptible to carcinogens.

Breast lobules become type 3 after the 32nd week of pregnancy. Type 4 lobules are formed after childbirth and produce milk. Both of these lobule types are resistant to carcinogens, thereby lowering the risk of breast cancer.

This information is not commonly given to young women who are seeking reproductive counseling. There is much said about "CHOICE"; why can't these women be allowed to make an "INFORMED CHOICE"? As it is, the choices that they make may well have serious consequences.

As you've seen from previous chapters, the evidence for creation and for a Creator God are hard to miss, unless of course you have a vested interest in denying His existence. It is useless to deny the obvious. God is real, denying His existence won't make Him go away. The day will come when you meet Him face to face. Will He call you friend, or say "I never knew you"?

Marriage was instituted by God Himself and intended to be for life. Today 50% of marriages in the general population end in divorce. For those who marry between the ages of 20 and 25 the divorce rate is 60%.

More than 50% of all marriages are preceded by living together. We've all known couples who say that they want to live together "to be sure that they can make it" as a married couple. The dissolution rate of those who cohabit before marriage is nearly 80%. Cohabitation is nothing more than an excuse to have sex without getting married.

God has a better idea. First choose your mate wisely. Then do your best to see that your relationship grows stronger, deeper and lasting. It's called, "marriage," and it is sanctioned by your Creator God Himself.

The cold hard truth is that the single greatest determiner of poverty is single parenthood. Children from single parent households are more likely to follow mom, (or dad), into a life of poverty, drugs, crime and promiscuity. You may not want to hear that but it's what the statistics show. And mom, if you are having guys stay over at night while your kids are in bed, think of what you are doing. Those kids may not be old enough to know what is going on but some day they will figure it out. They will know that different guys are around overnight. One day they will learn about the birds and the bees and all at once they will realize, "my mom is an alley cat!" What you will have taught them is that it is okay for a guy to exploit a woman by having sex without any commitment to them. Is that what you want your children to learn from you?

There I am on my soap box again. But face the facts: someone needs to wake this nation up to the truth that God is your Creator. He has every right to make the rules, this is His world. God's rules are not to limit your enjoyment. They are to keep you safe, happy, and fulfilled. He created you and knew exactly what is best for you.

There can be no greater joy then to be in God's will. He knows what you were created to enjoy doing. Still, people think that if they follow God's rules, they are going to miss out on something. THEY ARE RIGHT! If they follow God's rules, they will miss out on spending the night in the drunk tank. They will miss out on a lot of broken relationships. They will miss out on contracting one of those sexually transmitted diseases. It is good to miss out on those things that your loving Creator wants to protect you from.

Genesis 2:24 states: "For this reason a man will leave his father and mother and be united to his wife, and they will become one flesh." God is not speaking only of the physical union but also a spiritual bond which by His design was to bind the two together INSEPARABLY. Turn to First Corinthians 6:16: "Do you not know that he who unites himself with a prostitute is one with her in body? For it is said, 'The two will become one flesh." Sex is NOT simply a physical act, and the lingering bond, even though it was unintended by the individual, will last a lifetime. One-night stands can have detrimental consequences for years to come.

As we open the subject of "soul ties" we must understand what the soul is. Your soul is your mind, your will and your emotions. It is what and how you think. It is what you want and how you feel. Good soul ties are helpful, even necessary to your wellbeing. Bad soul ties are destructive.

From the research that I have done on the subject of "soul ties" it appears that the first sex partner that a woman has will have a form of dominion over her. This is not surprising: Genesis 3:16 says: "To the woman he, (God) said, 'I will greatly increase your pains in childbearing; with pain you will give birth to children. Your desire will be for your husband, and he will rule over you." Please don't miss the fact that this is what God Himself said. By design there is a bond between a woman and her first; (and subsequent) sex partner (s), one that has the potential to be a controlling factor in her life. Do you still wonder why women stay with abusive men? Statistics say that women who try to leave an abusive lover will try seven times before they stay away from him. Too often a woman will die before she severs a bad relationship.

Not all soul ties are bad. Hopefully we have good soul ties to our parents and siblings. We should have at least a few good close friends as well. We all need to have these good loving bonds with other people. The unfortunate fact is that we also have bad soul ties as well. These bad soul ties can be formed by personal relationships, by vows or commitments that we have made or through sexual relationships or any level of intimacy.

Before we get into the method of breaking these soul ties let me state that there can be such ties to persons whom you have not been physically involved with. It is possible to lust after someone to a point which you develop a soul tie to that person. Matthew 5:28 says; "But I tell you that

64

anyone who looks at a woman lustfully has committed adultery with her in his heart." He may also have created a soul tie with her.

So, what is one to do about these "soul ties" when they are preventing us from having a fulfilling relationship? PRAY! Of course, if you are not a believer this probably is not going to help. You'll need to get right with God first. Thankfully, God is waiting to welcome you and forgive you.

It would be helpful to have a Christian counselor, pastor or a close friend who is a committed Christian help you pray through this matter. This is not something that can be done in a few minutes. Depending on how many persons are involved and the depth of the soul ties, this is likely to be a time-consuming task.

First of all, your heart MUST be clean before God. You will need to confess all ungodly ties to the Lord. You must repent and make a commitment to the Lord to end all relationships that are not right in His eyes. You will need to be accountable to someone who can help you to keep this commitment. You must pray in the name of Jesus Christ to renounce and break loose from all ungodly soul ties and unhealthy bonding. Use the names of those persons, (if you know them), and ask the Lord to forgive you for damage that you have caused in those lives. Admit to God that you have sinned against these individuals.

Next you need to ask God to forgive you for sinning against your own body. You are His property, God created you for a special purpose. You should ask the Lord to forgive you for breaking His laws. Put the Lord at the center of your life. When you put the Lord at the center of your life, you are under his Devine protection. Put the right people in your life and let go of the past and leave those things behind.

No one loves you more deeply than God does. He is willing to heal your broken spirit and restore your soul. Don't allow your past to destroy your future through soul ties or demonic subjection.

To learn more about the subject of soul ties I recommend the book; "Untangle" by Terri Savelle Foy. It is available at terri.com.

What, you may ask has all this got to do with "the verdict?" Everything! We live in a fallen world where the majority of people do what they think is best for them with no consideration for what God wants from them.

You have seen in earlier chapters that God's Word is true and can be relied upon for wise guidance. Therefore, the verdict is: God created the earth, the sea, the plants, the animals, the people, and the universe in six 24-hour days. This was done about six thousand years ago and there will be a one-thousand-year reign of Christ to follow.

Sometime soon, the church will be taken out of the way so that the final seven-year tribulation can begin. Because the majority of people still want to go their own way these last seven years will be a time when it will be obvious to many that they need to accept Christ. Then there will be a "last round-up." The Scripture makes it clear that those who become believers in those days will likely be martyred. That would still be much better than the fate that awaits the rest of mankind, eternity in hell.

The greatest tragedy is that hell was never intended for people. It was created for the devil and his angels. Unfortunately, people who follow the devil rather than God will be sent to hell. It's a case of "follow the leader." You will spend eternity with the one whom you follow. I know that many people don't believe in a literal place called hell. They think that a loving God would never send them to such a place. They are right in thinking that God would not send them there; God has done all He possibly can to prevent it. It is not God; but your own choice to not accept the free gift of salvation which assigns you to hell.

It has been said that the greatest trick that the devil has ever pulled was convincing the world that he doesn't exist. He knows that very few would be willing to worship him directly. But he only needs to entice you with a counterfeit belief system. He doesn't care what you believe so long as you don't accept Christ as your Lord and Savior. If you believe anything else, he wins your soul.

Way back in 1965 commentator Paul Harvey gave what has turned out to be a prophetic speech. It was titled: If I were the Devil." If you would like to hear that commentary, just put, "Paul Harvey 1965 warning" on your computer search line, you will get dozens of hits.

Mr. Harvey began by explaining what he would do, if he were the devil, to take control of the world. He would, by any means possible, take over the United States of America. He outlined his methods as follows, (paraphrased).

He would whisper as he did to Eve that she should do as she pleased. He would tell young people that the Bible is a myth and that it was man who created God. Isn't this what is being taught in public schools? There is no better way to take control of any society than to indoctrinate the young with your philosophy.

He would make what is bad seem to be good and tell everyone not to be too extreme about religion, patriotism, or morality. He would cause people to look to the government for their welfare. He would make immorality the standard for T.V., movies, books and magazines.

If he were the devil, he would cause labor unions to do less work as idle hands most often work for the devil. He would increase the use of alcohol and recreational drugs and put an end to discipline in the schools. Just look around, these things have been going on for a long time.

As the devil, he would put atheists in the highest courts and get ministers to agree with their godless decisions. He would promote pornography and evict God from all public places. In the churches he would substitute philosophy for religion. Man would then be smart enough to produce super weapons, but they would lack the morality and wisdom to control them.

He would then take from those who have and give to those who wanted, thus killing the incentive of the industrious. At that point the police state would force everyone back to work. Mr. Harvey ends his commentary: "In other words, if I were Satan, I'd just keep on doing what he's doing."

Those prophetic words were broadcast on April 3, 1965. You can hear Paul Harvey's commentary online and you can read his entire speech. Unfortunately, we are all living that scenario in our daily lives.

CHAPTER 8

....

Why Are We Here?

T he single most important question one can ask is, "Why am I here?" What was I born to do? Is there meaning to this life or do we just live and die without purpose?

Jesus gave us the answer to that question in Matthew 22:36, "Teacher, which is the greatest commandment in the law?" Jesus replied: "Love the Lord your God with all your heart and with all your soul and with all your mind.' This is the first and greatest commandment. And a second is like it: 'Love your neighbor as yourself.' All the law and the Prophets hang on these two commandments."

The law and the Prophets are the Holy Bible. When you read the Ten Commandments you will see that the first four are about love toward God. The other six relate to love toward other people. You were created for a relationship first with God and then with others. You were designed by the same Creator God who spoke the world into existence. He had a specific purpose in mind for your life, yet few of us ever try to find out what we were created to do. The Psalmist, David wrote, "You knit me together in my mother's womb." David understood that God designs each person for a special purpose. In fact, we each have a "general purpose" as well as a "specific purpose." You are a person built for opportunity. You are unique, unlike anyone else, by God's design. Without Jesus, you are only a part of what you were created to be.

In general, we are all to take care of this planet on which we live. Should we all become radical environmentalists? NO, just environmentally responsible. We are to use the resources that we were given. They are here for our use. We are to use them wisely and leave our campground clean. For all the controversy over oil, I can assure you of one thing: we have all the oil that we will ever need. It's just in the wrong place politically. If we were allowed to go after the oil that we already know of in our own country, we would have all we need until God intervenes.

Each of us has at least one God-given talent. What is yours? Whatever it may be you can rest assured that God wants you to use it for His purposes. It will be something that you enjoy doing. God isn't going to have you doing work that you find boring. He loves you and wants you to enjoy each day to the fullest. God will stretch your abilities and help you to grow both spiritually and in your relationships.

As an example, let's say that you write songs for a living. You may or may not be getting rich at it. I'm not saying that you have to become a hymn writer. I firmly believe that if you let God inspire you, you will find a more fulfilling direction for your work.

In Ephesians 2:10 Paul wrote; "For we are God's workmanship, created in Christ Jesus to do good works, which God prepared in advance for us to do." The fact is that God has a job for you. What's that? You say that you already have a job! If what you are doing is not what God had planned for you, it will not be as fulfilling as what He had planned for you would have been. Read on to verse 3:20, "Now to Him who is able to do immeasurably more than all we ask or imagine, according to His power that is at work within us." Did you get that? God's power is at work in us; if we are willing to allow Him to. I don't know about you, but I can imagine some pretty big things. God can do "IMMEASURABLY MORE" than anything we are able to ask or imagine. Let's not miss the fact that He will do those things through us, if we will let Him use us. What could be more exhilarating than to have the very Creator of the universe empowering your every task?

Can't wait to get started? You must wait for His timing. I had been waiting to do one task that God had placed on my heart over five years ago. There was someone He had called me to reach with the saving knowledge of Christ, yet the door had not opened. It often seems hard to wait, yet I knew that His timing is perfect. A few months ago, I learned of something in that person's life that I could not understand. Later, when I could see the bigger picture, it made perfect sense. More importantly, had I not waited for God to open the door I might well have made a big mistake that would have been costly, if not impossible to rectify. God was working in the other person's life too, and He knew when they would be ready to hear His truth.

I learned of a half marathon that was to benefit a Christian school that I knew of. "That's great," I thought, "but I am 320 miles away what can I do?" Still, I couldn't help but keep thinking about this half marathon. There was no reason that I could not make arrangements to participate. I knew that the person that I had been trying to reach for Christ would be a participant too. Suddenly I could see many long-term prayer petitions being answered due to my saying yes to one appeal. Soon after I began training for the event God began to show me that He was with me and ready to assist me so long as I was willing to put forth reasonable effort myself.

Please don't miss that point! You MUST take a step of faith and begin doing what you can, then God will help you to do things that you could never do on your own. God helped me with the physical part of my commitment as soon as I began the training program. Within the first two weeks of training, He also made the money that I would need for the financial part of my commitment available from a source that I had not considered.

Is my task with this individual completed? No; not as yet. But God is in control and is working with both of us. I have long since learned to trust His timing. The reason that I mention this now is that you also need to learn that lesson so that you will not make the mistake of getting ahead of God's timing.

A great example of someone getting ahead of God's plan is Abraham and Sarah. God had told Abraham that he would be a father and that his offspring would be beyond number. But God didn't say how soon this would happen. After years had gone by and they were both old, Sarah told Abraham to take her slave girl and have a baby with her. In their attempt to solve one problem they caused more problems, and it hasn't ended yet.

Hagar, Sarah's slave had Ismael who is the father of the Arabs. As you know the Arabs hate the Israelites who are descended from Isaac, the son born of Sarah. Isaac was "the son of the promise." In Genesis 22:2 God said, "Take your son, your only son, Isaac, whom you love, and go to the region of Moriah."

In that verse God is not even considering Ishmael to be Abraham's son. This has been a great point of contention between the Arabs and the Israelites to this day. In the Arab world the first-born son is of great importance. In their minds, Ishmael was the first-born son of Abraham. He was first born by several years but, he was the illegitimate son. Ishmael was born of a slave, not the legal wife of Abraham.

After all these centuries the whole world is still at unrest due to the warring factions between these two half-brothers. This will continue until the return of the Prince of Peace, Jesus Christ. I hope that you are now able to understand why it is important to wait for God's timing. Okay, let's continue with what we are here for.

We are here to serve God; most people don't know that and even fewer take it seriously. To set the matter straight, there is nothing that we can do to save ourselves. Even when one decides to accept Christ as their Savior, it is the work of the Holy Spirit which leads you to that decision. You may ask, "What about good works? Doesn't good works count for my salvation?" NO! NOT ONE BIT! You can't do enough good works to earn ten seconds in heaven. Salvation is a free gift. If you could earn it, it wouldn't be free. What you can earn are rewards, but we shouldn't get caught up in trying to earn rewards. We are to do good works because it is the right thing to do. Don't you care about your neighbor? There are people all around you who don't know the truth of Christ. There are many ways to show the love of Christ to those around you.

What was the last thing that Jesus said before He returned to heaven? "All authority in heaven and on earth has been given to me. Therefore, go and make disciples of all nations, baptizing them in the name of the Father and of the Son and of the Holy Spirit, and teaching them to obey everything I have commanded you. And surely, I am with you always, to the very end of the age" (Matthew 28:18- 20).

That is known as "the great commission." It commissions all believers to spread the gospel everywhere in the world. Its main thrust is to save lost souls; after all, nothing could be of greater importance than their eternal destiny.

At the beginning of this chapter, I mentioned that we are to take care of our planet. We are responsible for protecting our environment, using the resources that are here wisely, and recycling what can be recycled. I was into those things before it was the "politically correct" thing to do. That was because I understood that this was a part of God's plan for mankind.

Oil; let's use it wisely while we are developing alternative power sources. Unfortunately, there are those among us who prevent us from using oil that is readily available for political reasons. This has caused the greatest hardship on those who can least afford the additional cost of fuel for homes and transportation. It has also put our national sovereignty in jeopardy. We must buy our much-needed oil from our enemies. Without enough oil our economy would collapse. Again, I say let's perfect new ways of doing business, but in the meantime, don't kill the goose that is laying those golden eggs.

But aren't our carbon-based fuels destroying the atmosphere? That depends on whose science you are looking at. If you recall that famous "hockey stick graph" of Al Gore's you'll remember that the story was that when the carbon dioxide levels go up an increase in temperatures followed. Guess what! When you move those graphs together and line up the dates you will find that it is the carbon dioxide levels that follow the temperature increases, just the opposite of what we have been told.

Recently there have been a number of scientists who have admitted that they had manipulated the data which was used to "prove" global warming. It is always easier for a scientist to get a grant to study a "crisis" than to get funding for something of little consequence. This tends to cause them to create emergencies which they simply have to study.

I really don't mean to offend anyone; it's just that I believe that we need to examine the evidence and find what is true, then act on the finding. I'm all for doing what is necessary, but let's be sure of our facts and not cause greater problems by taking the wrong actions. It is scientific fact that increased carbon dioxide levels help plants to grow bigger and better.

Why don't we have nuclear power? Other countries use it without any problems. As it turns out, Three Mile Island wasn't nearly as bad as we were told it would be. When "doomsday prophecies" don't materialize, it never makes the news. In the meantime, we must use oil and coal to power our electric plants. Some are looking to "plug-in" cars that won't use gasoline. At the other end of that plug there must be a coal powered generator. In effect the choice is petroleum powered or coal powered vehicles.

Let's get back to the main topic. We are not to be CEOs of His church; that is those who attend at Christmas and Easter only. You really need to be serious about your spiritual growth. Christianity is not a religion but a relationship. We should live as though Jesus is always close by, because He is. You need to attend at least one worship service each week and a group Bible study would be helpful as well.

You should have a set time every day to read your Bible and pray. I don't mean that prayer is a once-a-day thing. We can and should pray any time that a need comes to our attention. It is best when one can start the day with prayer and Bible reading. Because of the great importance of this I will give you more detail.

Why should you pray? Doesn't God know what you need already? That's drawing a wrong conclusion from a correct assumption. God wants to hear from us. That is how we develop our personal relationship with Him. He sometimes may answer you while you are praying. In mid-sentence you might realize that you need to change your petition. I've been there, done that. And in those moments, it was when I understood that God's way was right.

A few years ago, I had an uncle who had been admitted to the hospital; again. This had happened several times in just a few months. Each time I would pray for his recovery. I can never forget the evening that I began to pray for his recovery and suddenly the words would not form. In that moment I knew that what I intended to ask was not in God's will, I needed to change my request. It was then that I asked, "If it is his time to go, let him go easily." He died peacefully.

James 5:16 says that "The prayer of a righteous man is powerful and effective." Prayer is our response to God's invitation to work in partnership with Him. It's not about changing God's mind, but rather, it is to conform our own mind to His will. This is where we build our faith and trust in the Lord. He always answers your prayers. The answer may be yes, or it may be no. Sometimes the answer is, "wait." At other times He has something better for us. Yes, God often does give us what we ask for because he loves us and the people and situations that we care about.

I don't want to be like those who try to "sell Christ" to the unbelievers. Yes, absolutely there are many benefits to accepting Christ as your Savior. But don't be surprised if the devil works overtime trying to trip you up. As a Christian you are not immune to trouble. Just as lifting weights builds strength, working through problems, prayerfully, will build your faith. No pain, no gain is just as applicable to spiritual matters as it is to physical ones.

What do I know about trouble? Do I know the pain of loss? While I was still a teen my dad died. He had always seemed to be strong and healthy. His sudden death from a heart attack was a shock to everyone who knew him.

It was years later that mom was diagnosed with cancer. Her declining health kept her death from being a shock, but it was still a loss none the less. Numerous aunts and uncles, cousins, in-laws, and close friends have also passed away over the years. There is also my first wife who died quite suddenly after ten and a half years of marriage. More recently as you will recall from chapter one was the loss of "our little girl," Lisa. When it comes to the pain of loss, I've earned a Ph.D.

It is true that gold and silver are refined by fire. Yet I know that when I go through those spiritual trials by fire it is not because God is refining a lot of gold. He is just removing a lot of dross.

When you accept Christ, the devil will do his best to discourage you. Know this; the devil cannot steal you away from Christ. It would seem that the phrase, "once saved, always saved," comes from the Baptists. Whatever its origin it is absolutely true and Scriptural. When you are "saved" you are sealed by the Holy Spirit who will be with you at all times and in all situations.

We are here on this earth to serve our Creator and to get to know Him in a personal way. God picks all the wrong people to work for Him. He doesn't pick the brightest, the most charismatic, and the best-looking people. He picks those who are willing to do what He asks of them, even if it may be difficult or unpopular.

Remember those disciples that Jesus called to learn from Him and then carry on His work after He went back to heaven? Only Luke, the Doctor, had advanced education. Later on, Paul who had extensive theological education, was called into Christ's service. None of the others had much education, yet they were willing to do whatever was asked of them. They had three years of on-the-job training and those twelve men launched Christianity to the world.

We are here to learn to love our Creator and to get to know Him intimately. Serving Him by helping others is a hands-on way to grow closer to our Creator. Second Peter 3'9 states: He is patient with you, not wanting any to perish, but everyone to come to repentance." That doesn't mean that everyone will turn to the Lord, just that it is what He would like. It is why we all should be doing whatever we can to lead our friends to that "saving knowledge" of Christ while there is still time to do so.

We are here to serve Christ by serving others. This is not a one-way kind of service as the Holy Spirit is with us, to guide and help us in everything. We can count on God's help because He loves us.

There is no better example of God's love for us than is found in Luke 15:11-32. This is the story of the "prodigal son," but it is also about us. As you know, the story begins with a young man who asks for his share of the family fortune so that he can live as he pleases.

After a time, the young man runs out of money and when he comes to his senses, he wants to return home.

We all have at some time and in some way left our Heavenly Father and gone our own way. But when we come to our senses we too can come home to the Lord. Do you question His willingness to take us back? The story continues: "But while he was still a long way off, his father saw him and was filled with compassion for him; he ran to his son, threw his arms around him and kissed him."

Yes! God will welcome you home because He loves you as a father loves his son. As the story continues the father throws a party to celebrate the return of his son. The son is accepted back, fully restored to his place in the family. If you have walked away from God, know that He wants to restore you too. That is the reason that Jesus told that story, so that you could know the depth of His love for you.

This book will not contain all of the answers. It is intended to help you find the reliable Source for the most important answers that you will ever need. It will hopefully be your "Vector," pointing the way to your spiritual destiny. It is to instill a desire to seek God's purpose for your life and to build a personal relationship with Jesus.

CHAPTER 9

....

What Will Happen Next?

As we saw in previous chapters, we can rely on the Scripture to tell us the truth. We can also expect those predictions for the future to be just as accurate as those in the past. So, what's next?

If you're thinking in terms of earthquakes and volcanism, there is enough of that going on now. What about pestilence or disease? We have illnesses now that were not heard of only a generation ago. The prophecy that intrigues me most is found in First Thessalonians chapter 4:16-17, it is often referred to as, "the rapture."

Let me state right off that the word "rapture" does not appear in the Bible. That is only one of the reasons that I, personally, did not believe in the rapture for many years. Also, there are passages that talk about the persecution of the saints. That didn't seem to fit with the idea of a removal of the church from all the trouble that was said to come on the earth.

So, what do you do when your inquiring mind wants to know? Check it out for yourself and see who is right. I know many people who believed in the rapture, and these were well studied individuals. I knew that they wouldn't just accept the rapture without good solid reason.

In First Thessalonians 4:16-17 we read: "For the Lord himself will come down from heaven, with a loud command, and with the voice of the archangel and the trumpet call of God, and the dead in Christ will rise first. After that, we who are still alive and are left will be caught up together with them in the clouds to meet the Lord in the air. And so, we will be with the Lord forever."

Some read that mention of a trumpet and get confused over the use of trumpets in other passages. This has nothing to do with those other trumpets. When is this to take place? It could happen at any time. We have been told that it is imminent; and there is nothing that has to happen before this prophecy is fulfilled. We need to re-think that understanding of Scripture and will shortly.

As I have mentioned, I had a problem with the fact that there are references to persecution of believers during the tribulation. Upon closer examination I have found that there will be a large number of people who will accept Christ during the tribulation. These are the ones who will be persecuted in that time. The church will be removed because as stated in First Thessalonians 5:9, "For God did not appoint us to wrath but to receive salvation through our Lord Jesus Christ."

Furthermore, the "saints" must be removed from the earth before the antichrist can be revealed. They are the ones who "restrain" evil. This is why the "rapture" is needed. Second Thessalonians 2: 7-8; "For the secret power of lawlessness is already at work; but the one who now holds it back will continue to do so till he is taken out of the way. And the lawless one will be revealed, whom the Lord Jesus will overthrow with the breath of his mouth and destroy by the splendor of his coming."

The "lawless one" is a reference to the antichrist. He has been restrained to a great degree by the Holy Spirit who indwells all believers. When the church, (believers), is raptured, there will be no more restraint of the evil that the antichrist intends to do. The church cannot exist without the presence of the Holy Spirit.

For those who are unsure of this rapture business, you could just wait to see if a few million people vanish from the earth. The problem with doing that is that you would be putting your eternal destiny in jeopardy.

In writing about "what will happen next" I must turn your attention to Matthew chapter 24. In the third verse the disciples ask Jesus, "Tell us," they said, "when will this happen, and what will be the sign of your coming and of the end of the age? (N. I. V).

Notice that there are three questions in that verse, although the disciples thought that it was all connected. The first question was concerning the destruction of the temple. Jesus had just predicted that in the previous verse. The second coming and the end of the age are not one single event ether. Eschatology would place the two remaining questions at opposite ends of the tribulation. The "end of the age" would refer to the "church age," which will end with the rapture. The second coming will be when Christ returns at the end of the tribulation, seven years later.

Between now and the rapture, society will continue to become more ungodly. We can see this happening already. Our own government has passed many laws which are not "Scripturally correct." Abortion and same sex marriage, forcing God out of public places. Do you think that God will allow these things to continue? Unless we turn this nation around very soon, we will face the same end that other nations which rejected God have. They become crime ridden and poverty stricken, and their infrastructure decays.

Matthew 24:37 says; "As it was in the days of Noah, so it will be at the coming of the Son of Man" (Jesus). What was it like in the days of Noah? Genesis 6:5 says; "The Lord saw how great man's wickedness on the earth had become, and that every inclination of the thoughts of his heart was only evil all the time" (NIV). This is a picture of the world that we live in today. But you may ask if there are any other reasons to think that we are near the "end of the age."

YES! Scripture says that "God declares the end from the beginning." What does that mean? In Genesis we read that God created everything in six days and rested on the seventh day. First of all, God could have created it all in six minutes or even less if He wanted to. Second, why did He rest on the seventh day? Was He exhausted from all that work? I don't think so. Could it be that He was setting a precedent?

Where does the idea for a seven-day week come from? A year is the time it takes for the earth to travel around the sun. A month is the time it takes for the moon to go around the earth. A day is the time it takes for the earth to make a complete revolution. But why are there seven days in a week? Why not eight? Why not ten? In Biblical times it was the custom to work six days and have a seventh day Sabbath. This was based on the seven-day creation week. Yet I, and many others, believe that there is another reason for the seven-day week. As I said earlier, God declares the end from the beginning.

Remember that I said in chapter five that there is no valid scientific reason to believe that the earth is more than six thousand years old. Using Bible chronology, the Old Testament covers about four thousand years, and it has been two thousand years since the New Testament times began. Second Peter 3:8 says, "But do not forget this one thing, dear friends: With the Lord a day is like a thousand years, and a thousand years is like a day." If God were using that symbolism in relation to the amount of time He would give man on the earth, the seventh day, a day of rest, would correlate to the thousand years (millennium) in which Christ will reign.

What follows is the "scary stuff" found in the book of Revelation. It would be far better to be counted among the "saints" who will be raptured, removed from the earth before the great tribulation which is to follow. I would suggest that you rent or buy the movie, "Left Behind," and see if you really want to take a chance on experiencing the great tribulation first hand.

Frankly, things that are going on right now in our world make me wonder if this book will make it to print before God pulls the plug on us. It seems that the whole world has turned its back on Israel, God's chosen nation. The Arab nations want to destroy Israel. But we can be confident that God will not allow that to happen.

I receive daily e-mails from a man who spends much time in Israel. He meets face to face with the leaders of those mid-eastern nations. The situation there is very serious. You never hear of the full extent of the warfare that is going on every day in Israel. Our liberal news media is not interested in the plight of God's chosen people. What we do know is that Iran is enriching uranium, a step toward building a nuclear weapon. When such weapons become available to Iran, Israel will have no choice but to engage in preemptive action.

You must recognize that Israel is a small country, surrounded by enemy nations. From 1948 to 1973 they fought four wars. I believe that the reason those nations which hate Israel have not started another war is because Israel has nuclear bombs. Israel has adopted a policy called "The Samson Option." They have taken preemptive action against enemies who were building weapons of mass destruction. They are willing to deal a fatal blow to any enemy who would attempt to take over their land. Israel must defend herself. They have no other choice.

What has this to do with what will happen next? Most who believe in the rapture say that it is "imminent." It could happen at any time. They say that there are no other prophecies which need to be fulfilled first. That's not exactly true. I will agree that we are likely very close to that fulfillment, but let's dig a little deeper into the Scripture and see some other scary stuff that is predicted to happen.

Read the 24th chapter of Matthew and if you take it for what it plainly says, (and you should). You will see that Jesus doesn't mention the rapture until the last three verses. He speaks of "wars and rumors of wars" but adds, "The end is not yet." Jesus tells of the beginning of sorrows." To learn about these "sorrows" we need to turn to the Old Testament. When reading Old Testament prophecy, we find that there is no timeline. Things are out of chronological order as well as being hard to understand.

Isaiah 17:1 "An oracle concerning Damascus: See, Damascus will no longer be a city but will become a heap of ruins." That hasn't happened! Damascus not only is still there but it is the world's oldest city. Some Bible commentaries say that this prophecy was fulfilled in 732 B.C. by Assyria, (2 Kings 16:9), but Damascus was not totally destroyed at that time. Prophecy is often dual in fulfillment. If Israel has to "Nuke" Damascus, that will fulfill the prediction in Isaiah 17.

Something not mentioned in Isaiah 17 is found in Psalms 83:2-5. "See how your enemies are astir, how your foes rear their heads. With cunning they conspire against your people; they plot against those you cherish. 'Come,' they say, 'let us destroy them as a nation, that the name of Israel be remembered no more.' With one mind they plot together; they form an alliance against you."

Who would these nations be? They would include Iraq, Iran, Jordan, Lebanon, Palestine/Gaza, Saudi Arabia, Syria and Turkey. Iran is trying to become a nuclear power. Syria has a stockpile of weapons of mass destruction. Where did they get them? If you will recall the liberal news media loved to say that there no WMDs in Iraq. Of course not. They had all been shipped to Syria I'll take the high road and not mention what Bill Clinton was doing while those WMDs were being moved. Think back.

There was an earthquake in Syria in those days. Soon after there were caravans of semis hauling huge loads of "emergency aid" from Iraq. What kind of emergency requires missiles? Semi-trailers of that size are only used to hide and transport weapons.

The fact of those WMDs being moved into Syria is documented and well known. Still our news media has only recently mentioned it by accident. I have read the words of a former Iraqi General who has confirmed that those weapons were moved from Iraq to Syria in that way, and at that time.

Perhaps more important than what will happen next is when will these things happen. The Scripture makes it very clear that we cannot know the exact timing of God's prophetic plan. No doubt you have heard of others who set dates for the end. The time came and passed, and nothing happened. Jesus said plainly: "no one knows about that day or hour, not even the angels in heaven, nor the Son, but only the Father." (Matthew 24:36).

God knows human nature. If He set the date and told us when the end would come, we would do our own thing until that day arrived. We are to be doing His work until that time comes, whenever that might be. The 25th chapter of Matthew tells two parables which are directly related to the end time. Both show that there will be those who will not be doing His will and will receive the consequences.

In the parable of the ten virgins, we are told that five had planned ahead and were ready for the return of the bridegroom, a picture of the return of Christ. Five had not done as they should and were left behind, just as many will be at the rapture.

The second of these parables is about the three men who were given "talents." In that culture a talent was a sum of money equivalent to over one thousand dollars in our times. Still, that parable is better understood if you think of these talents as "abilities." The issue is, what are you doing with whatever talent God has given to you? Each of the three men had been given a different number of talents. They in turn were rewarded according to what they had done with the gifts that they had received. The man who didn't do anything with his talent lost even what he had been given. You definitely don't want to be like him.

I'm glad that Jesus said that "only the Father knows." It means that I don't need to try to figure out when the end is coming. What I DO need to do is WATCH. If you will read on in the 24th chapter, 42nd verse, (and you should), Jesus said, "Therefore keep watch, because you do not know on what day your Lord will come." The 24th and 25th chapters of Matthew give us plenty of reasons to be watching. Obviously, if He told us to watch there are things to be watching for. Back up to the verses 6-8 of the 24th chapter. "You will hear of wars and rumors of wars but see to it that you are not alarmed. Such things must happen, but the end is still to come. Nation will rise against nation, and kingdom against kingdom. There will be famines and earthquakes in various places. All these are the beginning of birth pains."

Does anyone care to guess why that passage mentions nations and kingdoms? Sure, some nations have kings and others don't. But I want you to realize that in reading the Bible you have to keep thinking. What are we to learn from this passage? What is its context? I believe that the mention of kingdoms does not mean earthly kingdoms but rather the kingdom of darkness, (Satan) against the kingdom of light, (God). There can be no doubt that there is a great spiritual warfare going on everywhere we look.

I checked my Nelson's study Bible on that idea, and it says that this passage "seems to indicate wars on a broad or worldwide scale." That doesn't mean that I was wrong or that Nelson's is wrong. What you should learn from this is that there are many things to consider as you study God's Word. You will never know all that can be learned. 2 Timothy 2:15 tells us to: "Do your best to present yourself to God as one approved, a workman who does not need to be ashamed and who correctly handles the word of truth." Get yourself a study Bible and a good concordance and use them.

Now if you want to look at that 9th verse of Matthew 24, just hold on. That begins a series of verses about Israel. Remember, the Bible is a book about Israel. It is about the Jews. Any other nation or people who are mentioned anywhere in the Bible are only mentioned in relation to the Jews or Israel. Verse 15 speaks of an event that cannot happen at the present time, but that will change soon enough. What we should take note of is found in verse 32 to 35. Jesus said; "Now learn the lesson from the fig tree; As soon as its twigs get tender and its leaves come out, you know that summer is near. Even so, when you see all these things, you know that it is near, right at the door. I tell you the truth, this generation will certainly not pass away until all these things have happened. Heaven and earth will pass way, but my words will never pass way."

What generation was He speaking of? Not the one that He was addressing on that day. Think about what else He said, he spoke about "the fig tree." That is a symbol of the land of Israel, and that nation disappeared for a time, only to be reestablished in 1948. This is the generation that will still be here when the things that He was predicting come to pass. In May of 1948 I was only five years old. I cannot say that I witnessed the re-birth of the nation of Israel because I was too young and lived on another continent. There were many my age who did witness that event, and today they would be around seventy years old. How much longer do you think these people will be around? This is the generation that will not pass away before the return of Christ. That generation is still here, but they are growing old.

The enemy nations which surround Israel will not rest so long as Israel exists. They want to divide Jerusalem, which is God's city. Make no mistake: God will not allow these enemy nations to succeed.

Still to come: there will be a new temple built in Jerusalem. That could not possibly happen today as the Dome of the Rock stands where it presumably should be built. To some that seems to be an insurmountable problem. Yet there are at least a few possible answers. It may be that the Anti-Christ will allow the temple to be built when he comes to power. There have also been some who question the proper location of the temple. Whatever the final outcome of that issue, it will be a moot point for those who are born again believers. They will have been taken away in the rapture by that time. I hope that you will be among them.

I am sure that certain things which are happening now affirm that we are drawing close to the time of the rapture. While the Republicans are trying to understand why Obama was re-elected, the reason is clear to me. It's not because of the low information voters. It was not because of the conservatives who didn't vote this time. God sets up kings and kingdoms. He also takes them down. These United States are going down because we have rejected God's rule.

What does that mean for those who try to follow God's will? They will be alright, God will take care of His people and there may still be a few years before the rapture takes place. This is no time to be unsure of your salvation.

What will transpire in the meantime? Economic problems will abound. Will there be any economic good news? Yes, there will be some growth industries. The administration will need to find new sources of revenue as the economy declines. Although Obama hates the oil and natural gas industries, he will allow hydraulic fracturing (fracking) because he can require dozens of permits and licenses at high dollar fees as a way to increase revenue.

There is enough natural gas to be a major export item if it could be loaded on ships as cargo. We don't have the facilities to do that. Natural gas would have to be liquefied and special ships would have to be built. It appears that the best investments would be in the industries which supply the equipment for oil and gas production and transport.

CHAPTER 10

....

What Must I Do?

I f you are a "born again" believer in Christ, you have already made the first move. You are "saved", and your eternal destiny is secure. Stay in the Word and do what you can to help others find the saving knowledge of Christ. We who are saved are in the minority. Most of your neighbors, even many who call themselves Christians, are in jeopardy. Understand that being "saved" is only the first step on a life-long journey.

If you ARE NOT a Christian, I pray that you will take the message of this book to heart. Christianity IS NOT A BLIND FAITH! The Holy Bible stands the test of truth. Only the all-knowing Creator of the universe could have dictated the information that is contained therein.

Is Jesus the only way to heaven? I'm sure that we've all heard that old "straw man scenario." What about some man in a remote land who has never heard the name of Jesus?" First of all, in such a case I know that God knows exactly what that person knew and how he conducted his life. God will be just. But that's not the reason people ask that question. They are trying to find a loophole. In their mind there has to be more, than one way to get to heaven. THEY ARE WRONG!

God, through Jesus, created this world. It's His ball, and He makes the rules. Jesus Christ is the only one who could, and did, pay the price of your sin. THEREFORE, He is the only possible way to gain entry into heaven. Let's not forget: you have heard the name of Jesus. You have heard that Jesus is the only way. Knowing this, you have NO EXCUSE for not checking it out for yourself and acting accordingly.

Hang on while I climb down off of my soap box.

The definitive answer to the question, "What must I do" is found in Acts 2:38. Here the apostle Peter answers that very question. "Peter replied, 'repent and be baptized, every one of you, in the name of Jesus Christ for the forgiveness of your sins. And you will receive the gift of the Holy Spirit.'"

First of all, you must believe that Jesus Christ is the Son of the living God. I don't mean that you simply acknowledge that there was a man named Jesus. You need to be sure that He is who He says He is, the very Son of God. You need to recognize that you are a sinner, and that Jesus Christ has paid the price for those sins, DEATH.

Next you need to be baptized. In the Scripture, every time someone was baptized, they went down into the water and were immersed. That means, all the way under the water. If sprinkling were all that was necessary, they wouldn't have had to go down into the river or lake to do the job. Let's cut to the chase. The Greek word, from which we get the word baptize, means "to immerse."

Baptism is symbolic of Christ's death, burial and resurrection. You are lowered beneath the water as a symbol of His death and burial. You are then raised out of the water as a symbol of His resurrection and your new life as His redeemed friend. The Scripture tells us that those who believe and are baptized will receive the Holy Spirit. This "indwelling" of the Holy Spirit is to help you to live the Christian life. We still have our own free will and we mess up far more often than we care to admit, yet we remain "His."

I should insert a word about temptation here. Temptation is NOT sin. It is only when you yield to temptation that you have sinned. Scripture tells us that Jesus was, "tempted in every way, just as we are – yet was without sin." (Hebrews 4:15). Turn also to the book of Matthew chapter 4: 1; "Then Jesus was led by the Spirit into the desert to be tempted by the devil." Note well as you read those verses that with each temptation Jesus responded by quoting Scripture. We need to be able to do the same. We, (hopefully) will not be speaking to the devil face to face as Jesus was, but we should be able to recall Scripture that fits the situation that we find ourselves in.

As a new Christian you should be telling your friends and relatives what you have discovered about Christ and salvation. You should also be in contact with other believers who can help you in this new journey that you have begun. We all need to keep learning, praying, and reading the Word daily. This is necessary so that you continue to grow in your understanding and your faith.

Do you have a G.P.S.? Just about everybody does. I keep mine in the center console of our Impala, (I never use it). I plug it in about once a week to keep it charged. We have something much better than a G.P.S. for our spiritual journey. It is the "vector" that we can totally rely on: the Bible. I cannot stress too strongly the need to read your Bible.

In John 5:5 Jesus asks a question to which the answer would seem obvious. "Do you want to be well?" One would think that this paralytic certainly wants to be able to walk. Why did Jesus have to ask such a question? When this man's mobility is restored, he will no longer be able to beg, he will have to get a job and earn his living.

Spiritually speaking, do you want to be well? Do you want to be forgiven and eternally saved? Sure, you want to be forgiven and escape eternity in hell. But do you want to serve the Lord because of that healing? Whatever you do for Him, the Holy Spirit will help you.

Christianity is NOT a religion; it is a relationship with Christ Himself. Anything less is just another religion. If you are looking to some other spiritual leader, you must be very careful; they must be leading you toward Christ. Let's cut to the chase; if people can't tell the difference between you and the world, (those who are not saved), you may be "saved," but you will have no rewards.

1 Corinthians 3:13 – 15; "his work will be shown for what it is, because the Day will bring it to light. It will be revealed with fire, and the fire will test the quality of each man's work. If it is burned up, he will suffer loss; he himself will be saved, but only as one escaping through the flames."

There are those who want to believe that they don't need to attend a church. The fact is, if you don't attend church regularly, you will drift away from the faith and God in a short time. There is a human propensity to drift. Drifting away from God is inevitable if we are not proactive. One must be in God's Word daily. We need to find a Bible believing church and become an active member.

How does one find a "Bible believing" church? Ask a leader of the church if they believe that the Bible is the inspired Word of God. There should be no hesitation in affirming that it is. Ask if they believe that God created the world and all that is on it in six 24-hour days. If they don't say yes, they are calling God a liar. They must also agree that Jesus is the Son of God and that the only way to be saved is through Him.

I do not intend to tell you to join with any particular denomination. As mentioned earlier, my family was Evangelical United Brethren, (E.U.B.). That denomination joined with the Methodists in the 1960s, but I never considered myself to be a Methodist. It is not that I oppose them; I simply was looking for a better understanding of God's will for my life.

I have no problem with the Presbyterians. In fact, I have studied many of the works of the late D. James Kennedy. He was indeed a Godly man and had great Biblical understanding. I do note, however, that they sprinkle, rather than immerse.

When we visit my wife's family, we attend the First Baptist Church where she grew up. Their doctrine is nearly the same as that of the New Testament Christian churches, (nondenominational). There are only two notable differences. In our church we observe communion every week. The Baptists do not. In the New Testament church, the baptismal pool is always ready for those who wish to accept Christ.

The Nazarenes also have sound doctrine, as do the Pentecostals, although I wish they would read what Paul had to say about speaking in tongues. It is not the name of the church that is important. What counts is the desire to follow God's will, to serve His people, and to lead the lost to the saving knowledge of Christ.

You may have noticed that I did not include Roman Catholics in my list of potential good churches. They have the same problems that caused Christ to denounce the leaders of the Jews. There are long lists of man-made doctrines which they insist must be followed while ignoring Scriptural issues. Nowhere did Christ authorize praying to His mother or any other human being. Scripture calls celibacy "the doctrine of demons." Bowing to idols is also prohibited. There are many more indiscretions.

It is not my words that will bring you to that saving knowledge of Christ. I can only present the facts of real science and Scripture in a way that you, hopefully, can understand. It is the Holy Spirit, speaking to your heart, Who will convict you and lead you to Christ.

I really need to say more about the need to attend a good church. In Hebrews 10:24-25: "And let us consider how we may spur one another on toward love and good deeds. Let us not give up meeting together, as some are in the habit of doing, but let us encourage one another – and all the more as you see the Day approaching." We all need to have other believers around us so that we can encourage each other. We are to love one another, and that mandate is second only to loving Jesus with all of our heart.

Believers should assemble together to worship their Creator and Savior. Doing this lifts our spirits and strengthens our souls. We meet to learn from the Word of God. Our goal should be to gain a deeper understanding of the Scripture so that we can avoid doctrinal errors. You may have heard of the "name it, claim it" gospel that is popular in many churches today. Do not be deceived! That is not based on sound scriptural interpretation.

We need to play an active role in your church to fulfill the Great Commission. You won't necessarily need to go to some foreign land. You can do a lot right in your own neighborhood. Of course, you can also support foreign missions with prayer and financial gifts.

Above all I must mention your "spiritual gifts." God has given all of us at least one spiritual gift. Many will have several of them. As a church member, you will be able to discover and develop those gifts to their full potential. For those who are not familiar with the term, "spiritual gift," these are your abilities, your strengths. Things you like to do.

As you develop your spiritual gifts and your service to others you will find that your faith will grow as well. You would do well to read the eleventh chapter of Hebrews which is known as the faith chapter. Everything that we experience works to develop our faith, and faith pleases God.

Let's not be confused about works. You are not saved BY good works. You are saved FOR good works. We should never be satisfied with anything less than God's best for us. That means that we should diligently seek to serve the Lord through whatever gifts he has provided to us. He will empower you to do all that He asks of you, but you must take that first step.

So, how does faith work for one who has lost a daughter? This I know beyond question. If I were to dwell on our loss I could sink into a state of depression and never accomplish what God has created me to do. I will always miss Lisa, her smile, her laugh, even things that she would do that

I would rather she didn't do. There are many of life's joys that she missed, but also pains and sorrows that she will not need to experience either. I have no doubt that she is in heaven where there is no pain or sorrow.

When evil happens, it doesn't mean that God doesn't love us anymore. God is love! He can't stop loving us and still be who He is. God is in control. We won't always understand what He allows to come into our lives. But there is a Devine purpose for everything that He allows to happen. When Joseph's brothers sold him into slavery it seemed like a bad thing. Years later, Joseph could tell them that what they had meant it for evil, God meant it for good, (see Genesis chapter 45).

Scripture seems to indicate that our eternal, individual roles will not be assigned until after the rapture and subsequent distribution of rewards. What we will be doing in eternity is not clear. This is probably because we have no earthly experience to compare it to.

What should we be doing now? Allow me to answer that with another question. What needs do you see in your community or your country? There are many more needs to be met, or problems to address then any of us can deal with. Pick any need that you are passionate about and do all that you can to deal with that need.

A lot depends on what our own government does about Israel. At present we are not standing with Israel in their time of great need. This puts these United States in danger of God's wrath. The machinery for our destruction is already in place by the directives of our own leaders. We are on the brink of economic collapse. Those who are at the helm, so to speak, of our government have ignored the constitution and set in place programs that make business too risky for those who would create jobs. They are making the cost of energy too high. They are destroying the best health care system in the world. We will soon find that "free health care" costs far more than we can possibly afford.

Update: As I write Prime Minister Netanyahu has requested a meeting with President Obama. That request has been denied. Campaigning and golfing are more important than world peace. This is not the first time that Obama has snubbed the Prime Minister of Israel. It has been made clear that the purpose of the meeting was to be in regard to Iran's nuclear program. It is clear that the administration has refused to take serious and significant action against Iran.

If America chooses to stand on the sidelines- or even worse, actively hinder Israel from doing what must be done, we are placing ourselves on the wrong side of God's prophetic Word. God has made an eternal promise of blessing for those who bless the children of Abraham. If we instead curse Abraham's children, we will be under God's judgment.

What must we do? We must do all that we possibly can do to restore limited government to this land. I will not tell you what to do other than to get informed of what is happening and act on that information in a responsible manner.

One thought that has been on my mind is the fact that there are some women who reject Christianity because of one passage found in Ephesians 5:22. "Wives, submit to your husbands as to the Lord." This is taken out of context. The 25th verse says, "Husbands, love your wives, just as Christ loved the church and gave himself up for her..." In the full context, the Scripture places an awesome responsibility on the man in regard to his wife. And that passage in First Corinthians 14:34 which says that "women should remain silent in the churches" is for that culture, not ours. In those days women were not educated nor were all men. This is not the case in our culture and there are many Godly women of great Scriptural understanding who teach the Word of God correctly. It is only in the Christian world that women enjoy equality and respect from their men. Christ Himself always treated women with respect and dignity. Even those who we might think were not respectable. He is more concerned with what you can be than what you have been. That goes for both women and men.

As I draw close to the end of this book, I cannot help but believe that when it has been turned over to the publishers I will think of other things, like the above paragraph, that I should have said. There will be things that I will think I could have said in a better way. Still, I know that I have tried to be true to God's Word and His Will in all that has been written. The final result will not be an eloquent work. But I sincerely hope that it will be a "VECTOR" which will guide many to the saving arms of Jesus. I pray that it will help many who know and love the Lord to understand Him better; and to be more able to show others the truth of Christ.

We have examined prophecy and seen that only a being who was outside of time and is all knowing could have dictated the Bible with such accuracy. Prophecy in effect is God's signature, endorsing His Word so that no one can deny His Devine authorship.

We have searched the geologic evidence and found that the only place that the geologic column can be found is in the textbooks. We have seen that the Biblical view which includes a great flood best explains the geologic evidence that we find all around the earth.

We have looked into the biological evidence to find that nowhere are there any upward evolutionary advances in life forms of any kind. Every change that we study is due to the loss of genetic information. That is the opposite of evolution.

The fossil record which Darwin hoped would prove his theory has in fact disproved the theory of evolution. The fossils show an explosion of many types of creatures followed by catastrophic extinction of many species. This is exactly the opposite of what evolution requires. The Bible explains this evidence very well.

With these facts in mind, we can see that the Bible is indeed the "Vector' that we need to guide us through our lives. Unless you were born a Jew, you need to turn to Jesus and become a Christian. Yes, the Jews will need to find their "Messiah" who is of course, Jesus Christ.

It doesn't matter who you are or what you have done, God loves you. Know that God loves you like a parent loves his or her own child, unconditionally! Yes, there are penalties for sin, but God still loves you because God is love. Turn to Him. Commit to Him. Do your best to live for Him. The very Creator of the universe longs to have a deep, personal relationship with you.

There remains one final story that I wish to share with you. This story actually happened nearly two centuries ago. I can think of no better way to rest my case.

On December 6, 1829, George Wilson and James Porter robbed a United States mail carrier in the state of Pennsylvania. They were soon captured and tried for this and other crimes and were both sentenced to hang until dead. The sentences were to be carried out on July 2, 1830.

Mr. James Porter was hanged on that date but some of George Wilson's friends pleaded for mercy from President Andrew Jackson. A formal pardon was issued by President Jackson and the charges resulting in the death penalty were dropped.

George Wilson, for reasons never explained, refused to accept the pardon. The court tried to force him to accept the pardon, but Wilson would not comply. The case reached the Supreme Court and the Attorney-General said: "The court cannot give the prisoner the benefit of the pardon, unless he claims the benefit of it... It is a grant to him: it is his property; and he may accept it or not as he pleases."

Chief Justice John Marshall wrote the following decision:

A pardon is an act of grace, proceeding from the power entrusted with the execution of the laws, which exempts the individual, on whom it is bestowed, from the punishment the law inflicts for a crime he has committed... "A pardon is a deed, to the validity of which delivery is essential: and delivery is not completed without acceptance. It may then be rejected by the person to whom it is tendered; and if it be rejected, we have discovered no power in a court to force it on him."

George Wilson committed a crime, was tried, found guilty and sentenced to death. Although he was granted a full pardon, he chose to refuse it, and be hanged.

NOW, dear friend! Know that God's Word says that "All have sinned and fall short of the glory of God" (Romans 3:23). That means you, me, and everyone who is on this earth. We are all guilty and deserve what the Scripture calls the second death; eternal separation from God in a place called hell. We all need a pardon from someone of high authority.

Praise God! We can have a pardon if we will only accept it from the One who created us, Jesus Christ. Our sin debit has been paid in full. Our rightful punishment was born by the very one who gave us life; and who sustains us and loves us in spite of ourselves. But! Have you accepted His offer of forgiveness? Have you accepted His pardon? Don't hesitate, don't guess, don't wait until you get your act together. That will never happen. DO IT NOW! Time is growing short. The stage is set for the final events of our world to begin.

I hope to see you in heaven. Get your free pass to go there now, before......

The End

WHERE DO I
FIND MORE INFO?

The following are Biblical Creationist organizations. They have hundreds of books and videos as well as web sites with downloadable information.

Answers In Genesis   www.answersingenesis.org
Creation Studies Institute   www.creationstudies.org
Institute For Creation Research   www.icr.org

For more information about breast cancer contact:

Breast Cancer Prevention Institute.   www.bcpinstitute.org

"Breast Cancer Risks and Prevention" third edition, can be found online at the above web site. You can print out the 20-page report from that site.

Coalition on Abortion Breast Cancer article; "Criteria Met to Establish Causal Relationship Between Abortion and Breast Cancer" www.pinkmoney.org

For information on sexually transmitted infections contact: www.cdc.gov/std

You can also go to: www.pamstenzel.com and view her "Sex Still Has a Price Tag" lectures. Parts 1 through 6 are online in ten-minute segments.

I highly recommend the following:

"The Case for a Creator" Available as a book or DVD; by Lee Strobel.

"The Case for Christ" Available as a book or DVD; by Lee Strobel "The Case for Faith" Available as a 3 pack with the DVDs above.

"The Genesis Flood: The Biblical Record and its Scientific Implications" by Dr. John C. Whitcomb and Dr. Henry M. Morris, copyright 1961.

For other titles go to the creationist web sites listed at the top of this page.

For further spiritual understanding I recommend viewing online: "In Touch Ministries", with Dr. Charles Stanley and "Turning Point Ministries" with Dr. David Jeremiah.

www.ingramcontent.com/pod-product-compliance
Lightning Source LLC
Chambersburg PA
CBHW020323130626
46549CB00003B/984